Women in the
community

This volume has been edited by Marjorie Mayo in
co-operation with the Editorial Board appointed by the
Association of Community Workers:

Gary Craig
Paul Curno
David Jones
Marjorie Mayo
John Ward

Women in the community

edited by

Marjorie Mayo

Routledge & Kegan Paul

London, Henley and Boston

First published in 1977
by Routledge & Kegan Paul Ltd,
39 Store Street,
London WCIE 7DD,
Broadway House,
Newtown Road,
Henley-on-Thames,
Oxon RG9 IEN and
9 Park Street,
Boston, Mass, 02108, USA
Reprinted 1977
Printed in Great Britain by
Redwood Burn Limited,
Trowbridge & Esher
ISBN 0 7100 8384 X

Contents

Contributors

MARJORIE MAYO is a research/community worker for the Joint Dockland Action Group, concerned with participation in the redevelopment of London's Docklands. She was previously a Lecturer in Community Work at the University of Surrey.

ELIZABETH WILSON trained as a psychiatric social worker in 1962 and has been lecturing in social work at the Polytechnic of North London since 1973. A feminist and a socialist, she has been active in the Women's Liberation Movement since 1970.

ELIZABETH LAWRENCE studied sociology at the University of Kent, and after some teaching experience has worked as a research assistant at Newcastle-upon-Tyne Polytechnic, working upon projects on shop stewards' education, the role of white-collar shop stewards and the position of women workers in trade unions. She has been an active member of Newcastle Working Women's Charter Group since 1974.

THE ISLINGTON GROUP OF THE NATIONAL ABORTION CAMPAIGN was formed in 1975, in response to the James White Abortion Amendment Act. The group represents different sections of the Islington community and particularly of local women's groups and of the local labour movement.

VAL CHARLTON was a founder member of the Dartmouth Park Hill Children's Community Nursery. She has worked as a teacher. Since 1969 she has been active in the Women's Liberation Movement.

ELIZABETH URBEN worked for two years as a social worker in North Nottinghamshire and Derbyshire before studying for a year at Surrey University in order to gain her certificate of qualification in social work. As part of this course she undertook the study of child-minders in Camden. She is now working as a social worker in the London borough of Lambeth.

JAN O'MALLEY was involved with the Notting Hill Community Workshop as a founder member. She has recently been writing the history of

community action in Notting Hill with a research grant through the
Centre for Environmental Studies.

CYNTHIA COCKBURN was a journalist and is now a research worker based
at the Centre for Environmental Studies. She has also been involved
in the Women's Liberation Movement and in various community action
groups including a community press and newspaper in south London.

SHIRLEY FROST was a founder member of Mothers in Action. As a
result she has also been involved with a number of other voluntary
organisations in the field of economic, legal and social rights.
At present she is a student at the City of London Polytechnic. She
has one son aged eleven years.

JANET HADLEY has been involved in the Women's Liberation Movement
since 1969. For a year and a half she was Information Officer for
Gingerbread.

ANNE HARRIS lives and works in Camden where she is a founder member
of the local Gingerbread group.

JALNA HANMER is the Lecturer on Community Work at the London School
of Economics, a member of Camden Women's Aid support group and the
Finance Group of the National Women's Aid Federation.

ANGELA WEIR has been employed for the last three years as a community
worker at Camden Community Law Centre. With other members of the Law
Centre she helped start and is now a member of the support group for
Camden Women's Aid Centre. She has been consistently involved with
the Women's Liberation Movement and is a member of the WLM's campaign
for legal and financial independence for women, and on the editorial
collective of 'Red Rag', a Marxist feminist quarterly.

ANN GALLAGHER is currently a lecturer on the Goldsmiths' Community
and Youth Work Course. She has done community development work in
the Philippines and was a community organiser in the USA. She came
to London in 1970 and became involved in the Women's Liberation
Workshop. In this country she has worked as a community worker for
The Albany, Deptford, and for Lewisham Social Services Department.

Introduction

Why the juxtaposition of the two themes - women and the community?
The Editorial Board believe that the choice of content for this
third volume in the Association of Community Workers' series on
community work requires some explanation. We need to set out the
rationale for our selection of subject matter and to justify the
importance which we attach to the potential for cross-fertilisation
between the different themes. In addition, given the breadth of
scope of the material which could legitimately claim to be relevant
to either 'women' or 'the community', we have to explain how we
have limited ourselves to the confines of one volume.

To begin with the last point - we have chosen to ignore both the
history of feminism in Britain and the history of community work/
community development up to the immediate past, i.e. the last ten
years or so. This is in no way to belittle previous experience and
achievements or to imply that the present has no roots in the past.
The women involved in the great Glasgow Rent Strike in the First
World War, or the suffragettes involved with Sylvia Pankhurst in the
East London Federation (1) are only some of the better known figures
of a long history of organising by women around community issues.
Nor do we intend to imply that there is nothing to learn from the
better established women's community organisations.

But we have decided to concentrate upon organisations and campaigns which date from the more immediate past, because we would
argue that there are specific factors in common between the growth
of the present phase of the women's movement and the rise of community action in the late 1960s and early 1970s which warrant particular attention. Without going into detail, it would seem at
least worth mentioning some of these. First, they have roots in
common. Both arose as part of the revival of left-wing/protest
politics, after the end of the period of relative consensus of the
1950s. Their antecedents were in campaigns such as those in
Britain against nuclear arms and in the USA against the Vietnam
War, and in the simultaneous reawakening to domestic questions:
the 'rediscovery' of poverty (2) and of the problems of minority
groups - typified for instance by the Civil Rights Movement in the
USA. As Juliet Mitchell explains of the women's movement: 'In discussing the historical time at which it arose, we have to consider

contemporary radical or revolutionary movements with which it is in alliance or from which it broke: the student movement, Black Power, draft resistance, already existent sectarian groups and reformist women's groups, Third World Struggles'. (3)

Both movements are also very much urban phenomena in that they are linked to the increasing awareness of the urban crisis - the exploitation and the consequent social and political tensions to be found within the inner city. And both have had links with the development of another aspect of the political reawakening of this period - the student movement. In various instances key actors moved directly on from involvement in the student movement to attempts to put some of these ideas into practice in the women's movement and/or in community action. Both have therefore started in some ways as middle-class phenomena, although both have, of course, spread to involve much wider social strata. Initially they also shared a certain sense of distrust of traditional left-wing politics, both in theory and in practice. This sense of the limitations of established working-class politics (e.g. of the Labour Party) and of their organisations in the workplace (the trade unions) can in part be seen, at least in the case of the latter, as the perspective of those leftists who, by their very class and background, feel alien to and even excluded from effective participation in such forms of political practice. On the other hand, the emphasis upon the problems of incorporation and the deadening hand of internal bureaucratisation has led parts of the women's movement and of community action into experimenting with newer forms which have, in many instances, turned out to be more flexible and appropriate for those spheres in which they operate. The theme of organisational challenge to traditional politics emerges explicitly in various forms in several of the contributions - and implicitly in others (4) - together with the realisation in most of them, now, that ultimately the only way forward for both women's liberation and for community action is in a series of alliances with the mainstream of working-class politics and organisations - the starting-point, after all, of the Working Women's Charter Compaign. Here then, the women's movement and community action are to some extent, at least, converging with contemporary movements within the broad trade union and labour movement itself - the strengthening of grass-roots campaigns, for instance around 'charters' within various unions and the development of the left voice, as compared with the greater degree of political consensus which prevailed in the 1950s.

In addition to certain common roots in the history of this political resurgence of the late 1960s, the Women's Liberation Movement and community action also share the potential for a common theoretical ground. Both include wide divergences of theoretical perspectives, stemming from a range of different political positions. Although the single most coherent influence has been from Marxist thinking, this has certainly by no means been universally or even probably for the major part explicitly accepted in either movement; but in so far as writers in each movement do adopt a Marxist analysis as their starting-point, both then locate themselves as involved in struggles around issues of consumption and more particularly social reproduction, as opposed to the more traditional trade union struggles at the point of production. In this sense, then, both

define the significance of demands arising from family and community needs in these terms, i.e. of consumption and social reproduction - whether these needs arise out of issues of housing, or education, play or nursery provision. Both the women's movement and
community action also consider state involvement as a key element in
meeting these needs. This theoretical ground is spelt out by
several of the contributors - for instance in Elizabeth Wilson's
chapter 1 and by Elizabeth Lawrence - and much of this thinking
underlies other chapters, even where the authors would by no means
consider themselves in other ways, perhaps, to be Marxists.

On the other hand, from a comparison of the contributors' viewpoints, one can trace some of the reasons for the relative lack of
cross-fertilisation so far achieved between community action and
the Women's Liberation Movement (where these theoretical explanations have been more developed). Elizabeth Wilson, for instance,
raises this problem. Other chapters also deal, both in theory and
in practice, with the reasons for the relative lack of involvement
of women in community action, even allowing for the fact that in
principle this community field has been defined as precisely
women's sphere. In practice, it seems that the very reasons for
this definition, arising as they do from women's relative marginality in the alternative sphere of production - the workplace -
account for their all too frequent marginality in the sphere of
social reproduction in the community. In other words, the family
responsibilities - the dual role of the working wife and mother
which helps to reinforce her in the role of a marginal at work, as
part of the reserve army of labour (5) to be sucked in and out of
the workforce with the booms and slumps of the economy, are also the
forces which tend to reinforce her in her marginal role in her
other sphere - the community.

The attitudes and prejudices of both men and women which support
these stereotypes apply in the same way, of course. These are some
of the reasons why, for example, organisations so often feel they
have to be headed by men, at least in the prestige, as opposed to
the routine, positions - chairmen as opposed to minutes secretaries.
Ann Gallagher's chapter offers some practical explanations of why
these tendencies seem to appear more marked in some types of community groups than others - based approximately upon a distinction
between upper-working-class as opposed to less respectable and less
formally organised working-class organisations. These problems in
practice are also illustrated - for instance Jan O'Malley describes
the cases of two exceptional women involved in community struggles,
both of whom were forced into leadership positions by the very des-
peration of their situations. The chapters from 'self-help' organisations of parents on their own, Gingerbread and Mothers in Action,
provide further examples of the initiatives which women are often
forced into taking - although other chapters illustrate the eventually unbearable tensions that this situation can create - the pressures of the responsibilities of breadwinner and child-rearer as
well as of community leader - which can eventually force the single
parent, in particular, to give up her community involvement (the
supposed unreliability and marginality of the female worker reappear-
ing again, in the community setting).

The theme of women at work and at home and the links between

their roles in each is also treated from another aspect in the
chapters concerned with provision for the under-fives. Val Charlton,
for example, deals with the tensions and contradictions within a
community nursery project not just as they are seen by the different types of parents involved - although that is complex enough
when different social classes and different social needs are
involved - but also in terms of the viewpoints, needs and aspirations of nursery workers, also women who are typically exploited
and low paid. Elizabeth Urben's chapter on the problems of child-
minders in Camden discusses an even more extreme form of this question - minders being generally the worst paid and most exploited of
all workers involved in provision for the under-fives. Child-
minders are characterised by the most negative stereotype - yet
they are also women who are reinforced in a caricature of the
female role situation - particularly isolated and confined to the
home through their responsibility for several very young children.

A further aspect of the links between women at work and women in
the community is raised in the discussions of the role of the community worker - in particular the woman community worker. Elizabeth Wilson's chapter considers some of the issues which, she suggests, both women and men community workers have tended to skirt
around or avoid altogether. Ann Gallagher also offers some practical suggestions for remedying this state of affairs in the future -
that is, for instance, for avoiding collusion in reinforcing
sexist role stereotypes and hence the limitations on women's
involvement in community action which occur even in some organisations set up supposedly to further this very involvement. For
instance, she considers those women's groups set up by well-meaning
community workers that actually concentrate upon women as wives
and/or mothers, and which end up suffocating rather than facili-
tating the development of other facets of their personalities or
the full discussion of their other needs and aspirations.

Other criticisms of community and social workers are expressed,
too, apart from this all too frequent failure to relate their view
of themselves as women to their definition of their professional
role. For example, the failure to offer community groups real
support whilst genuinely accepting their autonomy is mentioned as a
serious obstacle to future co-operation. On the other hand, the
very diversity of the women's movement means that for social and
community workers there is no single solution to all these problems.
For example, two chapters on battered women's centres are included,
not just because they represent alternative and to some extent com-
plementary accounts of these centres themselves, but also because
they are symptomatic of wider divergences in women's community
action. The logic of the more feminist approach, for example, would
seem to allow little or no scope for alliances with other mixed-sex
community groups, or with male or even non-feminist women community
workers. Alternatively, the logic of the other approach would seem
to be that there may be considerable scope for alliances, and even
that these may be the key to the furtherance of struggles around the
underlying social and political issues involved. In building up
such alliances, given adequate sensibility to the particular women's
issues involved, the community worker would have as much potential
for offering support as in his or her work with mixed-sex groupings.

As in previous volumes, the editors have made it a matter of
principle not to attempt to mould the contributions made by these
self-help groups themselves to fit into the perspectives of the
professional workers. Rather, we have wanted these to stand in
their own right as statements coming from their own self-
definitions and standing upon their own ground. This approach
applies most obviously, for instance, to the contributions from
organisations such as Gingerbread and Mothers in Action, the
Working Women's Charter and the National Abortion Campaign. In a
more general way, it runs through the entire volume - all the
contributors are, after all, women, and even the more socially
advantaged will have to contend with at least some of the problems involved in being a woman, a wife and/or mother and an
activist at work and/or in the community. In this sense, then,
all the contributions are partisan, arising as they do from the
same minimum of common ground in the experience of these problems
as actually or at any rate potentially limiting and oppressive.

Yet the conclusion or at least the implication of the majority
of the contributions is that, nevertheless, women's issues in the
community are not ultimately capable of resolution apart from the
wider resolution of the entire framework of socio-economic
issues. The book as a whole, then, concludes not with a definitive
solution, but with an opening up of the discussion around these
issues which appear explicitly or at least implicitly in many of
the contributions - that is the questions of the potential contradictions between the short-term and the longer-term demands of women
in the community, and of the whole relationship between women's
liberation and community action and the broader struggles for
socio-economic and political advance in Britain and beyond.

References

1 See e.g. S. Rowbotham, 'Hidden from History', Pluto Press,
   London, 1973, for an account of this.
2 See e.g. P. Townsend and B. Abel-Smith, 'The Poor and the
   Poorest', Bell, London, 1965.
3 'Woman's Estate', Penguin, 1971, p.13.
4 See e.g. the chapter on the Working Women's Charter by Elizabeth
   Lawrence, Cynthia Cockburn's chapter and Jalna Hanmer's chapter.
5 See e.g. the concept developed by Karl Marx in 'Capital', vol.I,
   Progress Publishers, Moscow, 1965, ch.15.

1 Women in the community

Elizabeth Wilson

The time is long overdue to inject some feminism into the community
work scene. The growth of community work and the growth of the
Women's Movement both date in this country from the same period, the
late sixties with its upsurge of political consciousness; they have,
perhaps not surprisingly, kept apart, yet have often operated on the
same terrain, attempting to grapple with the problems of urban-
industrial daily life; in my view community workers have much to
learn from what the Women's Movement has done and what it has to say.

It is unlikely that a book such as this would have appeared five
years ago, and that in itself is a tribute to the inroads made into
consciousness generally by the Women's Movement. The Sex Discrimination and Equal Pay Acts represent a recognition by those in power
that feminist demands do speak for many women. On the other hand
the Women's Movement, going under the sneering label of 'Women's
Lib', has been consistently misrepresented, distorted and attacked
in the media, and this reaction is a measure of the fear generated
by militant women. Women's demands do, in fact, objectively, at
least in the short run, threaten men, for they seek an end to some
of the privileges from which men profit and exploit women.
Suffragettes even when they simply heckled male politicians at election meetings met with a response of exaggerated and grotesque hostility, physical cruelty and sexual assault (1) and today fear has
at times led to a hysterical negativism about the Women's Movement,
with the result that many men and women are confused as to what
feminism is actually about.

The Women's Movement today embodies 'emancipationist' demands for
women's rights; of its original Four Demands, formulated in 1970,
the demand for equal pay, the demand for readily available abortion
and contraception, for equality of education and job opportunity,
and the demand for child care facilities, all are concerned with
women's rights. In addition they involve recognition of the
obstacles standing in the way of equal access to employment - the
main ones, of course, being 'control over our own bodies' and child
care.

Yet the demand that women should control their own fertility and
the demand for the socialisation of child care also imply something
more than emancipation and civil rights; they point towards a

1

'liberationist' analysis, which locates women's oppression at a
deeper level than legal discrimination and perceives it as more
complex than straight economic exploitation. The core of women's
oppression is found in the family form which prescribes stereo-
typed roles defined rigidly along gender lines. This formulation
is often attacked by those who claim that it is out of date, and
that these days men do share in housework and child care; yet
studies (2) show that even though men help with the housework,
they still do much less than women, and that women retain the
responsibility for domestic chores and child care even when they
themselves are out at work. This analysis of women's oppression
within the family does not, as is sometimes suggested, imply a
crude strategy of 'smash the family' any more than a demand for
free abortion implies a hatred of children. It does demand that we
look beyond equal pay and civil rights, and indeed it suggests that
some of the seemingly reformist civil rights legislation cannot
mean very much until we understand more about the oppression of
women as it forms our very consciousness. The fifth and sixth
demands of the Women's Liberation Movement, added in 1974, point to
this deeper analysis. The fifth demand, the demand for legal and
financial independence (3) is concerned with the legal definition
of women as the dependents of men, as this manifests itself in the
tax and social security system, home ownership and tenancies and
many other areas. This is not a simple civil rights issue, but a
recognition of 'the way the State upholds the family in its present
form and, thereby, forces women into a position of dependence on
men'. (4) This suggests the question: Why should the state in
practice uphold female dependence, and points to the analysis of
women's unpaid work in the home as the cheapest way of reproducing
the labour force(s) for capital. The sixth demand, for an end to
discrimination against lesbians and the right of all women to a
self-defined sexuality, suggests - though rather confusedly - that
we must examine the whole nature of sexuality if we are ever to
understand sexism fully. This does not mean that the Women's Movement believes that lesbianism is the answer to women's sexual
oppression; it does on the other hand recognise its validity and
give it authenticity instead of treating it as a sickness or as
deviant.

Apart from the six demands and the campaigns connected with them,
there has been another persistent and important strand in the
Women's Movement, which perhaps relates more directly to the practice of community work; that is the whole area of what are sometimes called 'the politics of everyday life'. This too has implied
a concern with personal relationships, but also with the problems
of housing, social security and welfare with which community workers,
too, often have to deal. Groups of women squatting in unused property have both exposed the iniquities of the housing system and
tried to initiate new forms of collective living. Women claimants
have made persistent attacks on the harassment practised by local
DHSS offices and in particular have campaigned against the oppressive
cohabitation rule.

Thus, while one image of Women's Liberation sometimes pushed in
the media is that of middle-class women wanting more professional
status in middle-class careers, these groups of squatters and

claimants have in fact pointed directly to the intense oppression
suffered at every level by the hundreds of thousands of women
living at or near the poverty line (or indeed beneath it).   They
have revealed the ugly truth that for these women, perhaps even for
a majority of women, life in the early 1970s has remained a life
largely consisting of drudgery.

For men, even when they are unemployed, work remains the core of
their lives; certainly any political activity in which they engage
is likely to be at their place of work.   For women, on the contrary, even when they work, the home remains their sphere.   Their
work is likely to be organised in such a way that they can keep the
family routine going undisturbed, which means they are often forced
into low-paid, super-exploitative part-time work, into night-
cleaning or the 'twilight shift' - in which case the cost of keeping the home together and caring adequately for the children is the
marital relationship, which cannot be maintained in a relaxed and
happy way when interfered with by shift-work and extreme fatigue.
Small wonder that the divorce rate is rising.   The organisation of
work around domestic commitments also means that women are less
able to unionise than men; even when in full-time nine to five jobs
they are likely to have to rush home, rather than stay on for the
union meeting.   Men themselves demand this of women, and preferring
their own wives to be at home cooking the dinner, do not necessarily welcome other men's wives, still less single women, at their
branch meetings, often a form of male club anyway.   So, working or
not, the matters women care most about, or are responsible for,
happen at home.   That is, they happen in the community.

This brings me to a problem that deserves a much fuller treatment
than I can give it.   What is 'The Community'?   Social work in
general, including community work, seems to me to have accepted
this trendy label unthinkingly, in the most woolly way imaginable.
Community workers in particular have all too eagerly snapped it up
as though it were somehow radical.   'I'm a neighbourhood agitator,'
one student said to me. (Paid for by the state?) By now, however, the
initial enthusiasm has given place to a more realistic critique, (6)
although it is one that still fails to lay sufficient emphasis
on the community specifically as the place where women are.   Politically, the concept of 'community' is a confused one with roots in
Ruskin, Morris and Guild Socialism, in all of which was a strand of
romantic hankering for medieval life seen as more human and less
alienated than modern mass society; (7) yet this concept could, as
for instance in the work of Hilaire Belloc, (8) lead to a reactionary analysis.   Socialism, after all, can never be anti-modernist and
anti-technological in this simplistic way; Marx rejected (politically) 'the idiocy of rural life'.   Community development has,
nevertheless, usually been seen by planners as an opportunity to
recreate the spirit of the old working-class communities such as
Bethnal Green, the essential warmth and goodness of which has gone
unquestioned.   Yet the supportive spirit of those communities was a
defence against harsh conditions and class repression; simply to
bewail its passing is again an over-simplified reaction.   Juliet
Cheetham and Michael Hill, (9) in fact, have suggested that the
spirit of community dear to the hearts of middle-class planners is
a feature of middle-class rather than of urban working-class life
today.

A reading of the Seebohm Report (10) gives us rather a more
objective understanding of what the radical rhetoric has con-
cealed. On the one hand this Report recommended the rationalisation of existing welfare services into one large local authority
department and was thus a part of the continuing trend towards the
centralisation of the state bureaucracy, also to be seen in the
reorganisation of the NHS. This however represented more than just
local government rationalisation; it was seen as part of a
rationalised intervention by the state in family life; its
jumping-off point was the prevention of delinquency, and it saw,
as part of social work with families, the increased organisation
of the community as an additional and much needed reinforcement
of the social order. (11) This was spelt out quite explicitly in
the Seebohm Report: (12)

> The feeling of identity which membership of a community bestows
> derives from the common values, attitudes and ways of behaving
> which the members share and which form the rules which guide
> social behaviour within it. Such rules are the basis of the
> strong social control over behaviour which is characteristic
> of highly-integrated and long-established communities.
> Powerful social control may, of course, stifle the individual
> and produce over-conformity, but it has been suggested that
> the incidence of delinquency is likely to be highest either
> where little sense of community, and hence little social con-
> trol, exists, or where in a situation of strong social control
> the predominant community values are, in fact, potentially
> criminal. Such ideas point to the need for the personal social
> services to engage in the extremely difficult and complex
> task of encouraging and assisting the development of community
> identity and mutual aid ...

Seebohm, in other words, links the development of community work
with the preservation of family life.

Community issues are indeed of central importance to women.
The reality of community life, as opposed to the confused and
romantic dream-image is women living in a direct relationship to
the State as mediated through housing departments, schools and the
State welfare system which supports the family. The division of
labour within the family usually means that it is women who go to
the rent office, women who attempt to grapple with the schools,
women who are interviewed by the social worker. A large element in
social work consists of attempts to get working-class women to do
their job 'better' - they receive 'help' and advice in budgeting
and paying off rent arrears. Nor are community workers less likely
to perceive their job in these terms than straight caseworkers.
For example, last summer I had a student whose work in his community project placement was to set up a group for unsupported
mothers. He and his supervisor were in disagreement as to whether
there should be a separate play group for the children. Whereas
my student saw the group as an opportunity for the mothers to have
a break from the children with whom they were cooped up all day, so
that they could discuss their problems and their situation and perhaps come to see it in a different and less individualised way, his
supervisor felt differently. She felt that the mothers and
children should remain together, because 'we are trying to help them

to be better mothers - they hit their children and shout at them so
much.' Thus she did not see these mothers' behaviour in terms of
their own economic class position and their position as women, nor
did she have qualms in imposing traditional norms of motherhood on
them. Yet this same woman was the next moment passionately arguing
for community work as a radical alternative to repressive casework;
the fetish of method indeed.

When women are isolated with their children in the home, it is
difficult for them to organise collectively. Women have none the
less been the mainstay of local groups, tenants' associations, for
example, and of single-issue campaigns. Campaigns around safety
crossings on dangerous roads, for instance, are usually the work of
mothers whose children are at risk. Women predominate necessarily
in militant pensioners' groups, because women tend to live longer
than men. Women have organised nursery provision; they have
organised around family allowances; the National Abortion Campaign
is one aspect of an attempt to organise better health care for
women. This book offers the opportunity for a closer look at some
of these campaigns, most of which connect to the welfare sphere,
and a critique of the contradictions with which they are often
riven. Here I shall simply try to suggest some of the problems
they raise; and point to the positive aspects as well.

In a misguided and idealistic attempt to come to grips with the
political organisation of women in the community Selma James (13)
and Maria Rosa dalla Costa (14) could suggest nothing more con-
structive to campaign around than a 'wage for housework' - something that would surely lock the housewife yet more securely in
her isolation. This slogan appears to be attractive to some women
community workers. In general I think it a not unfair assessment
of the campaign Selma James has been trying to wage in this
country since 1972 to say that while it has achieved a good deal of
publicity and generated much debate, it has never attracted a large
following, and it has been rejected on a number of occasions by the
National Conference of the Women's Liberation Movement. The notion
of 'wages for housework' has however a certain immediate appeal,
although many women - housewives and working women, not just political activists - reject it equally sharply. Its analysis is based
on a Marxist conception of surplus value - women, according to
Selma James perform surplus labour (unpaid) for capitalism (which
she perceives in a rather conspiratorial light) - and she argues
that a demand for this work to be waged is somehow revolutionary.
At the same time much of the brunt of her attack falls on the
sexist and anti-women behaviour of men both in the trade unions and
in the home and she has always posed her campaign as an alternative
to the efforts of Trotskyist groups working within Women's Liberation to emphasise women at work above all else and to neglect the
housewife. Yet a wage for housework could not in practice challenge
the role assignment of home and child care that seems to many women
just as important as issues related to pay and wages. 'Wages for
housework' in the form of Supplementary Benefit allowances to
unsupported mothers, family allowances (much more generous in some
other European countries than in ours), and even some form of salary
for motherhood, already exist in capitalist society and have not
greatly improved women's position, and certainly have not

revolutionised it. Presumably in our society such an 'endowment
for motherhood' (which is what Eleanor Rathbone called it) would
be paid for by taxing wage-earners (the majority of whom are men)
and would therefore represent some form of income redistribution
as between men and women, would give women a 'right' to a minimum
income of some sort and therefore make them less immediately
dependent on their husbands. On the other hand it would surely
make men even less willing to share tasks in the home ('You've
been paid to do it, haven't you?'), and in the longer term the
idea of giving added importance to domestic work in this way
seems to lead right away from the much more progressive demand
for the socialisation of housework and child care. In a highly
advanced technological society it should not be necessary for anyone to do the sort of work many women still perform in the home,
and indeed some writers have suggested that domestic work represents a pre-industrial formation within capitalist society, just
as underdeveloped countries persist alongside capitalist ones.

Yet it is right to point to the isolated condition of the housewife, and community struggles can be one way in which this may be
overcome. It is true that militancy over one issue does not
necessarily lead to a higher generalised political awareness, so
that a highly active woman in a tenants' organisation may limit
her militance to this single issue; it may never lead her to a
more political understanding of the economic system that creates
housing problems any more than it may lead her to an understanding
of her own oppression as a woman; but this criticism is true also
of the trade union and wages struggle at the point of production -
many trade unionists, no matter how militant, are entirely reformist in their general understanding of the social conditions under
which they live. Yet it would be wrong therefore to condemn their
participation (or the participation of left-wing militants) in
these struggles.

There is, all the same, a danger that the sexual division of
labour is reduplicated in the political sphere, with men struggling
at the point of production while women fight the community struggles
on issues related to home life. It is also the case that in these
struggles women may see themselves as fighting for their families
or their children rather than for themselves, thus repeating the
self-sacrifice in the interests of the family traditionally demanded
of women. At least a woman involved in a struggle for equal pay
knows that she is fighting (a) for herself and (b) for other women,
and this is very important in raising her consciousness.

Another problem of the politics of the community is the tendency
for campaigns involving welfare to teeter towards welfarism themselves. This has been a besetting problem for the claimants' union
movement, for example, with claimant activists repeatedly finding
that they, like social workers and the CPAG, were seen as and became
'experts' who helped other people, when the claimants' unions were
intended to promote self-help and to enable an oppressed and poverty-
stricken group to stop relying on other people and fight back for
themselves. The same problem has been encountered by the women's
groups who have set up refuges for battered women all over the
country. These refuges have tried to give (and indeed have given)
the women who came to them a new sense of themselves and have helped

them to feel less weak and hopeless; at the same time the refuges
are mostly run or at least initiated by women who have not themselves been battered, and they are very conscious of the dangers of
becoming social workers. Perhaps on the other hand these dangers
have been overstressed in the Women's Movement of today. Political activity of whatever kind has always tended to involve activists in the individual problems and daily lives of those with
whom they come in contact; the accounts of Sylvia Pankhurst (15)
and Antonietta Macciocchi (16) attest to this; Doris Lessing (17)
encountered the same problem as a Communist Party activist in
East Africa. Perhaps it is a mistake to uphold too rigid a division between politics and care for the individual. The Women's
Movement has after all consistently stressed the political element
within personal relationships; and it is precisely bourgeois social
work (18) that has adhered to a rigid and sterile division between
'the individual' and 'society' or 'politics', and created or pro-
moted stereotypes of the political activist interested only in the
overthrow of society and ruthless in his attitude to individual
suffering, as opposed to the 'caring' caseworker whose heart is
swelling with pity for his fellow-men. It has been considered one
of the positive aspects of women's involvement in union struggles
that they do in fact raise issues of the social conditions of work,
instead of sticking to generalised economic issues, so that far
from being negative, involvement in personal problems may represent a higher level of political consciousness.

Community workers on the whole have however not even begun to
come to grips with these problems for the simple reason that they
have yet to reach a stage at which they understand that women suffer
from a specific form of oppression. They are of course aware - all
social workers, at least in local authorities are aware - that
women, and especially unsupported mothers, often lead dreary and
down-at-heel lives; social workers do know that for these women
poverty and isolation are likely to be crippling. As a response,
attempts to form 'Mums' groups' have become common. It is my
impression (but this is only an impression) that these groups are
usually set up with no clear idea as to what they ought to achieve.
Are they an institutionalised form of the suburban 'coffee-morning'?
Are they supposed to develop into action-orientated groups along
community work lines? Are they, on the other hand, supposed to
engage in some form of consciousness raising? Or are they supposed
to be educational in the way that Women's Institutes set out to be?
The social worker's liberal reply might be: 'Does it matter? They
can make it into what they want it to be', but this isn't really
good enough, because left to themselves the women might not have
made it at all; and, supposing that the women collectively decided
to ransack the social security office or barrack his boss at a
council meeting, the social worker might not only be very embarrassed, but in certain circumstances his job might be endangered,
so it is simply irresponsible to say, 'It's up to the women themselves.' I imagine that these groups are usually a well-meaning
attempt to help the women involved feel less isolated by intro-
ducing them to other women in a similar situation; social workers
are often bewildered and disappointed when the groups don't 'go
well' and may blame the women for their apathy and lack of

consciousness; yet it might be more meaningful for some of these women to seek work, while others may be looking for a new boyfriend rather than contact with a group of women as depressed as themselves. Others again may feel quite satisfied with a life that centres upon children and domesticity and resent an intrusion which implies that they should not be satisfied. It is not as if all women are feminists.

I have suggested elsewhere (19) that social work often reinforces the class gulf between women social workers and their women clients. I may have worn old jeans and a fly-blown tee shirt to visit my 'homeless mums', but I had a comfortable home to go to and a comfortable salary to spend on my many tee shirts and pairs of jeans. It is hard for some social workers imaginatively to grasp the extent of hardship faced by their clients, still less the particular forms of consciousness it generates. This has also been true of some activists both in the Women's Movement and in the claimants'. Just as some of the unemployed must have resented activists who railed against the 'work ethic' and demanded the right to live off social security (while they on the other hand hated the dependence on social security and were desperately looking for work), (20) so the Women's Movement style may sometimes alienate working-class women. It is fun to pick up period bargains at jumble sales only if you are rich enough not to have to; many working-class women hate a style that looks dirty and unkempt and regard jumble sales as the last shameful resort of those on the dole. The more you have, the less you need, and the less you have the sharper your pride.

Hardship is intensified in the present economic crisis when the government response to inflation is the classic double of unemployment and social services cuts. Unemployment among men (and women) means that women have to work harder in the home to make less money go as far. Cuts in social services mean an added burden to women. One form of economising in the NHS has been the premature discharge of patients, and this means more nursing at home for relatives (almost always women). It seems that at present one woman in ten is looking after sick relatives. (21) Cuts in ancillary services such as meals-on-wheels and home helps affect women in three ways; first, these services often go to OAPs, likely to be women; second, their withdrawal may mean more burdens on·the daughters of these old people; third, the services offered work to women, for these services relied almost entirely on both paid and voluntary female help. (22) Social disintegration and the breakdown of other services such as the educational system also mean more worry for mothers, for it is they who are habitually blamed for juvenile delinquency and truancy, and they who have to try to tackle both the schools and their discontented children. Collective action by parents to grapple with school problems does not appear to have been organised to any extent in working-class areas; where parents have intervened, as at Highbury Grove School and Tyndale School (both in Islington) where complex issues were at stake, the situation was distorted so that their intervention was made to appear reactionary and authoritarian.

Finally, what of the women who are themselves community workers? When community work first became popular there was a tendency to pose it as a form of radicalism hostile to traditional social work of the 'professional caseworker' variety. The image was of the long-haired young man, recently a student, opposed to a dowdy, conservative PSW or almoner, the Young Turks against the old maids. It has indeed been suggested (23) that it was the influx of men into social work generally and community work in particular that led to its new radicalism. Men are more radical than women, who tend to be conservative; so went the explanation. If there is any truth in this at all, simply to dismiss women as reactionary (and the author in question relates this supposed conservatism to women's biological nurturant role in the most traditional way imaginable, although a contributor to a book allegedly about radical social work) is to ignore the way in which they are trained from infancy to a role that stresses the personal and eschews militancy, politics or too much interest of any kind in the outside world. Nor has the intervention of radical male social workers been especially helpful to women in the community. For example, many of these young men were particularly interested in 'youth' - but this turned out to mean boys. Girls might be used as bait to attract the boys (who after all are the trouble makers who have to be 'integrated') to discos, but in general their needs have been neglected; young girls in fact remain one of the most pitiably under-provided for groups in our society. For some reason feminism was slow to catch on amongst women social workers. Some of the women who went into community work were radicals but not feminists, so that important feminist issues were unfortunately not raised at an early stage in the development of community work when they might have had maximum impact. There are now more feminists amongst social workers than there were, however; some of them choose to work in battered women's refuges, others bring to community work a new perspective; a few have chosen to work as feminists in the more highly professionalised maternity and obstetrics departments or with the mentally ill.

What is it then that community workers have to learn from the Women's Movement? In the first place that daily life is political - political in a deeper sense than most community workers understand. I think also that many feminist activists have shown a greater sensitivity and understanding about what women's lives are really like than have community workers, whose comprehension has often been as superficial as their goals have been unclear. Perhaps most important of all, the Women's Movement, whatever its difficulties and contradictory tensions, has demanded the right for women to speak for themselves. This has to be the first demand of all oppressed groups. Community workers must learn to listen to women, instead of telling them what they want, what they are 'really' like and how they should be. But in order to do that, of course, they will first have to realise that women are there - that they exist, out in the 'community'.

Notes

1   Sylvia Pankhurst, 'The Suffragette', London, 1911; Andrew
    Rosen, 'Rise Up Women', Routledge & Kegan Paul, 1974.
2   'Social Trends', HMSO, 1974; Michael Young and Phyllis
    Willmott, 'The Symmetrical Family', Routledge & Kegan Paul,
    1973; Red Rag pamphlet no. 1, 'Towards a Science of Women's
    Liberation', 1973.
3   The Women's Liberation Campaign for Independence (the Fifth
    Demand Campaign), The Independence Demand (obtainable from
    7 Killieser Avenue, London, SW2).
4   ibid., p.1.
5   Wally Secombe, the housewife and her labour under capitalism,
    'New Left Review', no. 83; see also Jean Gardiner, The role
    of domestic labour, 'New Left Review', no. 89; Margaret
    Coulson, Branka Magaš and Hilary Wainwright, Women and the
    class struggle, 'New Left Review', no. 89; John Harrison,
    The political economy of housework, 'CSE Bulletin', spring
    1974; and Angela Weir, The reproduction of labour power,
    'Case Con', spring 1974.
6   Roy Bailey and Mike Brake, eds, 'Radical Social Work',
    Arnold, 1975, ch. 8; also Gerald Popplestone, The ideology of
    professional community workers, 'British Journal of Social
    Work', 1 (1), April 1971; and also a number of articles in
    'Case Con', a Revolutionary Magazine for social workers,
    published by Case Con.
7   Raymond Williams, 'Culture and Society 1780-1950', Penguin,
    1961.
8   'The Servile State', London, 1911
9   Community work: social realities and ethical dilemmas,
    'British Journal of Social Work', 3 (3), autumn 1973.
10 Report on the Local Authority and Allied Personal Social
    Services, Cmnd 3703, HMSO, 1968.
11 Elizabeth Wilson, 'Women and the Welfare State', to be
    published by Tavistock Publications Ltd in late 1976, for an
    extended discussion of this and many of the ideas touched on
    in this article.
12 p. 15.
13 'Women, the Unions and Work', Crest Press pamphlet, 1972.
14 'The Power of Women and the Subversion of the Community',
    Bristol, Falling Wall Press, 1972. 'Red Rag', no. 2, 1972;
    ibid., no. 5, 1973, and Angela Weir and Elizabeth Wilson, A
    reply to Selma James, 'Radical America', 7 (4 and 5), Fall
    1973 (special issue on women's labour), all criticise the
    arguments of James and dalla Costa.
15 op. cit.
16 'Letters to Althusser from inside the Italian Communist Party',
    New Left Books, 1973.
17 'A Ripple from the Storm', Panther, 1973.
18 e.g. Brian Munday, What is happening to social work students?,
    'Social Work Today', 3 (6), 1973.
19 Women together, 'New Society', 14 September 1972.
20 Hilary Rose, Up against the welfare state, 'Socialist Register',
    Merlin Press, 1973.

11   Chapter 1

21   Hilary Land, personal communication; and see Red Cross to
     teach home care, 'The Times', 6 January 1976.
22   'Social Trends', HMSO, 1974.
23   Howard Jones, ed., 'The New Social Work', Routledge & Kegan
     Paul, 1975.

2 The Working Women's Charter campaign

Elizabeth Lawrence

INTRODUCTION

The first section of this chapter will discuss the relation between women's position at work and in the home. The aim of the analysis put forward will be to demonstrate the connection between exploitation at work and oppression at home. This context is essential for understanding the role of the Charter Campaign and the extent of social change necessary for the full liberation of women. The second section will deal with the role of women in trade unions, discussing the problems women face when organising in unions. The third section will analyse the direction of the Charter Campaign and the implications of the demands of the Charter and the political issues it raises. The fourth section will look at the development of the Charter Campaign. The fifth will deal with the work of the Newcastle Working Women's Charter Group. The final section will discuss the future of the Charter Campaign.

1 WOMEN AT WORK AND AT HOME

The problems women encounter at home and at work cannot be separated. They are part of the same process. A woman may be refused promotion or even a job because she is married and has children, or even because, as a woman, she may at some stage in the future marry and have children. Employers consider that women who have children are more likely to take time off work, e.g. if their children are ill (although these same employers also often regard it as a woman's responsibility to look after her children when this happens). They also pay women workers less than male workers so that economic considerations mean that if a parent has to take time off work to attend to children, that parent will be the mother. These employers also provide fewer training schemes, job opportunities and chances for promotion for women workers, so women workers have less reason to be concerned about keeping their jobs through good time-keeping and fewer days' absence.

The reader can multiply examples of these processes for herself/himself. But the overall result is that on the whole women get the

worst rewarded and least interesting jobs. And, important for any
attempt to struggle against this, this situation is connected to
women's role in the home. Women form over one-third of the working
population. Nearly two-thirds of the women who work are married.
In 1970 women's hourly earnings were 60.1 per cent of men's.
Women's wages have tended to stay around 60 per cent of men's. In
April 1975 the average male wage was £60.8, whereas the average
female wage was £37.4. (Both amounts refer to full-time adult
workers, figures from New Earnings Survey Estimates, April 1975.)
In other words, women form a large highly-exploited proportion of
the working class.

Another aspect of the problem is the number of women who do
part-time work. About 18 per cent of women workers are part-timers
and women constitute about 80 per cent of part-time workers
(Department of Employment figures, 1971). Part-time workers are
disadvantaged in terms of job security, holiday pay, sickness pay,
pension rights and any other similar benefits that full-time
workers may receive.

The fact that many women have to work part-time is frequently a
result of the lack of provision of nursery facilities for young
children. An even more severe problem is the lack of facilities
for school-age children during working daytime hours when school
has not begun or has ended, and during school holidays. One solution suggested to this problem is for a grandmother to take care of
the child if the mother is working. But grandmothers may be under
retirement age and may wish to work too, and it is no solution for
a woman to gain the opportunity to work at the expense of another
woman's opportunity.

Our society assumes it is the responsibility of the woman to
look after the children. The man, if sympathetic, 'helps' her.
For most couples there is no possible alternative because typically
the man can earn enough for the family to live on, whereas the
woman cannot. But in any case, equal sharing of child care within
the family is not an adequate solution. The nuclear family does not
provide a sufficient environment for the full development of young
children. What is needed is the creation of communal child care
facilities. To understand why this does not occur, we have to consider the structure of the family in capitalist society.

But before we analyse the structural relationships we have to
look at one other aspect of women's work situation. That is the
question of unemployment. If women work for pin-money, then it is
obviously just and fair that women workers should be the first
people to be made redundant and put on short-time working in periods
of economic recession and unemployment. If women are supported by
their husbands and if men have the duty to support their wives and
be the breadwinners for their families, then it follows that women
do not have the right to work.

To understand women's position at work and in the home, we also
have to discuss the role of the family. One essential tool of
analysis is the distinction between exploitation and oppression.
Exploitation is here taken to refer to the expropriation of surplus
value produced by workers at work. Oppression is taken to refer to
all other forms of suffering which also have their structural basis
in the capitalist mode of production. The rate of exploitation,

that is the rate of surplus value produced, is calculated by
determining the proportion of labour-time the worker spends in
creating sufficient value to reproduce his labour power (i.e. his
ability to work) and comparing it with overall labour-time. The
value the worker creates in addition is the surplus value the
employer receives. The value of the worker's labour power is
socially determined; i.e. it includes things beyond physical sub-
sistence, such as the means to maintain the worker's family, pay
for entertainment and whatever else the existing relation of
forces between classes requires.

I referred to the worker as 'he' in the above passage not through
some slip of the pen, but because the above theory does not fit
perfectly in the case of women workers. If the wage paid to the
male worker is sufficient for him to support a family; i.e. pay
for the reproduction of the next generation of the workforce, then
the value of the woman's labour power is correspondingly reduced.
Women's wages are based on the assumption that women will be supported by their fathers or husbands. Most women have little choice
except to be dependent on men or to accept a considerable reduction in their standard of living if they attempt to exist solely on
their own earnings. Women workers are not paid the full cost of
reproducing their labour power. The poverty experienced by
unsupported women with children is adequate indication of this.
It would appear that while historically the working class regarded
it as an advance for the male worker to be able to earn enough to
support his family, this has proved to be an uncertain benefit in
that it has disadvantaged women workers both vis-a-vis the employers
and vis-a-vis male workers. If the working class could reject the
goal of the family wage and replace it by the aim of an adequate
income for all workers, this would be an important step forward
towards the unity of male and female workers.

The financial dependence of women on men within the family also
flows from this. The family as an economic unit is important for
capitalism in a number of ways. It reproduces the next generation
of workers. It also provides a number of services for the male
workforce, for example, cooking, cleaning, washing and sex. These
are provided free in the home. The family also provides a source of
cheap labour (women workers) for capitalism. This is the role the
family structure plays in the working class. For the capitalist
class, the family also provides a channel for the inheritance of
private property. If a man is to pass his property to his son, he
has to be sure he is his son. This requires that wives have sexual
relationships only with their husbands. Thus an economic relationship leads to a repressive sexual morality. And this morality
exists not only for the capitalist class but for the whole society.
The family, therefore, is not only an economic unit. It has consequences for individuals who live in (or outside) families in
economic, social, psychological and sexual terms. The psychological
role of the family means that the family provides for the (male)
worker a pleasant escape from the workplace. The home becomes the
longed-for opposite to the work situation. In fact the polarisation
of the two is a consequence of alienation affecting all aspects of
existence under capitalism. If the home is a pleasant refuge for
the male worker, then this is achieved by the work the woman worker

performs in the home; the cooked meal, the tidied room, the warmed slippers and the quietened children. Thus home is a radically different experience for male and female workers. For the former it is a compensation for the unpleasantness of work, for the latter it is more work - although both may also perceive the home as an escape from the workplace. Indeed, many women workers aspire to be full-time housewives only to be driven to tranquillisers a few years later by the boredom of isolation at home and the difficulties of coping alone with young children.

2   WOMEN IN THE TRADE UNIONS

Our picture of the relation between capitalist society and the family cannot, however, be complete without considering the organisations that workers have developed in their struggles against capitalism, i.e. trade unions. If it is true to say that women's position at work cannot be understood without reference to the family, then the same is true for trade unions. Here we need to examine certain frequently encountered vicious circles. The trade union leader says that women do not attend meetings or take an active part in the union. He then does not bother to encourage women to attend union meetings and gives low priority to problems relating to women workers. So the women workers see that the union does not do much for them and wonder why they should attend union meetings at all (especially when they are held at awkward hours for women with children and the men do tend to laugh or to start talking if a woman should get up to speak). Then the union leader says that women are apathetic and do not try to help themselves. Women, however, form over 20 per cent of trade union membership (over two million women workers are trade unionists), and women are joining unions at twice the rate of men. Women are still severely under-represented as conference delegates and as lay and full-time trade union officials. Recently more women have been appointed as trade union officers either with special responsibility for women members or to general posts within the union. Where these women are sympathetic to Women's Liberation and the demands of the Working Women's Charter, there is a considerable role they can play in helping to reorient unions towards taking up the problems of women workers. There is, however, a danger of tokenism. If these women become statutory women, or if the other union officials assume that because the union has a women's officer then other officials need not concern themselves with the problems of women members, then these women will become so marginalised in the union structure or so overloaded with work that they become ineffective.

Sexism in trade unions arises in many aspects of union activity. At an obvious level it consists of failures to provide creches at union meetings and conferences or to arrange for the meetings to be held in working hours; of giving low priority to disputes affecting women members; of giving low priority to recruiting women (often this occurs because unions give low priority to recruiting in small workplaces where a greater proportion of women work). It also, and equally importantly, consists of discouraging women when they try to speak at union meetings, with patronising remarks and sexist jokes from male members and sexist forms of social activities organised by unions. Many trade unionists are quite unaware of the extent of sexism in their unions.

Trade unions, in addition to being permeated by the sexism of capitalist society, are also, as institutions, affected by bureaucracy. This adversely affects the participation of all members in the union. It is important to pay some attention to this problem, which has led to some debates in the Women's Liberation Movement about working in trade unions. Bureaucracy in trade unions arises from structural causes. It occurs first through a necessary division of labour. Because most workers work a thirty-five- to forty-hour week or longer, with overtime, they cannot work full-time on trade union activity. As trade unions developed they therefore started paying some members to work full-time as union organisers. This put these members in a relatively privileged position inasmuch as they escaped from unpleasant and monotonous work in industry to work full-time for the union. As the position of trade unions gradually became more established and more respectable, the trade union officials benefited correspondingly. In addition, as unions developed into large organisations, internal channels of communication and structure became formalised. This concentrated information and power in the hands of full-time officials. Bureaucratisation thus develops out of the way the working class has to organise under capitalism. Variations in union rules and structures do make for some differences in the degree of bureaucratisation; for instance in some unions, full-time officials are elected, in others they are appointed. Bureaucratisation is not unavoidable, but the only real guarantee against it is the full participation of the membership in union affairs. This is difficult for most members to achieve at all times, given other personal commitments.

It is necessary to analyse the roots of bureaucracy in order to combat it effectively. If the structural reasons for bureaucracy are not considered, it is all too easy to ascribe all sell-outs by union officials to the particular character of some individual or to the sexism which affects trade unions. An analysis of how to fight the bureaucracy is essential for working in the unions around the Working Women's Charter. This includes the need to fight for measures of workers' democracy within the unions, such as annual election of all officials; payment of all officials at workers' average wages; right of recall of officials; right of members to information about negotiations and all other matters which affect them; and guarantees that decisions about conducting disputes and particularly about ending them are to be taken by the workers concerned, not by the officials. If the Working Women's Charter Campaign can encompass these issues when it has to confront them, then working in the unions means taking up the demands of women's liberation among the social forces (i.e. the working class and its allies) which can create the type of socialist society which contains the possibility of women's liberation. Working in the unions does not mean giving into the political backwardness and present sexism of the trade union movement.

Many women ask, 'Why should we work in the unions?' In discussing the negative features of trade unions I have tried to indicate ways they can be combated. But in addition it is necessary to say

that trade unions, because of their organised strength, can play a
major role in assisting women's struggles. Women workers, like all
workers, need the support and collective strength of other workers
to win wage increases and improvements in working conditions and to
combat redundancies. In many disputes in which they as workers
become involved, they need support from other workers. Women
workers have traditionally been employed in small workplaces and/or
weakly organised workplaces. For such groups of workers outside
support is even more important. These points about solidarity are
accepted by many trade unionists nowadays. (In the past it took a
long fight to persuade trade unions to accept women as workers and
trade unionists.) What the Working Women's Charter means, however,
is that the benefits of the collective strength of the trade union
movement should also be extended to women who work at home and are
not unionised. If trade unions support campaigns for nurseries,
abortion and contraception, full social security rights for women,
and also support tenants' struggles, etc., then they support
struggles to improve the position of all women. There are various
possible practical points of connection, too; for instance, social
security workers could collectively decide through their union not
to implement the cohabitation rule; gas and electricity workers
could refuse to disconnect tenants; social workers could stop telling battered women to return to their men; doctors and nurses could
refuse to induce births when not medically necessary; media workers
could censor sexist material; tax officers could stop implementing
a tax system which discriminates against women and unmarried
people; teachers could campaign for more nursery schools. There are
many actions which groups of workers could take collectively which
would give practical support for the demands of the Working Women's
Charter and of the Women's Liberation Movement. Such actions by
trade unionists would benefit both other women trade unionists and
those women who work at home.
    In recent years there have been a number of campaigns and
struggles involving women. Among these were the NJACCWER (National
Joint Action Campaign Committee for Women's Equal Rights), the
nurses' struggles of summer 1974, Imperial Typewriters, SE1 and Win-
grove & Rogers (referred to also in other chapters in this collec-
tion). Their struggles are important in understanding the context in
which the Working Women's Charter Campaign developed.

3 THE WORKING WOMEN'S CHARTER

What is the Working Women's Charter? What is the role of the Charter
in organising around particular demands? It is essential to sort out
these issues before discussing in detail each of its component
demands. The Charter is a way of organising around some demands
towards Women's Liberation within the trade unions and the community
beyond them. What is important is the use of the Charter as a lever
for taking up these issues within the trade unions. Clearly there
can be much debate about the demands of the Charter and some of them
can be criticised as partial and inadequate. For instance it does
not contain any protests against the oppression of black women and
gay women; it does not include any provision for paternity leave;

the family allowance provision is not indexed to the cost of
living; the demand for abortion is not for free abortion on demand
provided on the National Health Service; there is no clause
against compulsory sterilisation; the demand for nursery provision
is not for community-controlled 24-hour nurseries; the Charter
contains no demand against redundancies. Still it is possible to
amend it and improve it.

In the early stages of the campaign, however, the problem was
that debates over the specific demands in the Charter could have
acted as a diversion from organising around it. What was considered important was to win some victories around its demands.
Without this basis, a Charter composed of the most advanced
demands, which would achieve complete liberation for women, would
still be a very hollow document.

On the other hand, the demands of the Charter, if won, despite
their limited nature, would still accomplish a considerable change
in the position of women and of all workers. For example the
achievement of a national minimum wage would radically alter the
position of low-paid workers; extension of child care facilities
would allow many women to work and to participate in unions and
would also allow more women to choose to have children if they
wished to without sacrificing financial independence; extension of
contraception and abortion facilities would have implications for
the development of human sexuality separated from reproduction;
and point no. 10, a change in women's position in the unions,
could restructure existing union organisation if it involved a
general struggle for workers' democracy inside the trade unions.
The demands of the Charter must be fought for not as a set of fixed
static demands but as a key to unlocking a whole process of
developing struggles round the issues contained in it, the central
issue of which is the relation between women's position in the
family and at work.

4 HISTORY OF THE WORKING WOMEN'S CHARTER CAMPAIGN

The Working Women's Charter was drawn up by a sub-committee of the
London Trades Council in spring 1974. Since then, it has been
accepted by many trade union branches and trades councils and some
trade union conferences. Many local conferences have also been held
on the Charter and been sponsored by trade union organisations.
Working Women's Charter groups have been set up in many towns and
cities. These groups, besides developing propaganda around the
demands of the Charter, have tried to organise support for local
struggles and campaigns involving women. A problem encountered by
several Charter groups has been that many trade unions have been
prepared to give token support to the Charter but not to organise it.
One way of tackling this problem is to set up women's caucuses in
the unions. These are composed of union women activists who organise as a group to see that women members are fully involved in the
union and that the union, as a whole, takes the question of Women's
Liberation seriously. These caucuses, therefore, should be the
exact opposite of the type of women's sub-committee the union
bureaucracy employs as a means of shunting all women's issues to one

side. A good example of this type of women's caucus is the Women in
Media Group which has established a code of practice on advertising
and other examples of sexist images in the media, and which campaigns against discrimination against women in the media. Women in
other occupations such as education, health and social work can
organise in women's caucuses around both working conditions and the
way their work is used to reinforce women's role in the family.

In 1975 two major developments occurred in the Charter Campaign.
One was the attempt to introduce restrictive legislation on abortion
in the Abortion (Amendment) Bill proposed by James White MP. The
Working Women's Charter Campaign was one of the organisations which
set up the National Abortion Campaign, and for many Charter groups
the abortion campaign became the main focus of activity for several
months. The other significant development was the rejection of the
Working Women's Charter by the Trades Union Congress conference.
The motion from the Society of Civil Servants calling for support
for the Working Women's Charter not only said that the TUC should
accept the demands of the Working Women's Charter, but also that the
TUC should campaign for the Labour government to implement the
Working Women's Charter and that the TUC should support any struggle
around the Working Women's Charter. If the TUC had accepted this
motion, they would have been committed to a real struggle around
the Working Women's Charter. This would have meant opposing the
policies of the Wilson government, particularly the cuts in social
expenditure, the wage limits and unemployment. As the trade union
bureaucracy were not prepared to do this, they had to see the
Working Women's Charter was defeated. They persuaded the TUC conference by a two-thirds majority to reject the Charter on the
following grounds: that the TUC were opposed to a national minimum
wage, and that the clause on abortion would offend some members.
The national minimum wage was opposed on the grounds of opposition
to statutory wage controls. The same conference, however, accepted
the Labour government's £6 limit on wage increases. The £6 limit was
voluntary only to the extent that the government would have imposed
statutory controls if the TUC had not accepted it voluntarily. The
real problem for the TUC was that the likely proposed national minimum wage would have been at least £30 (not a fortune, but a figure
Jack Jones of the Transport and General Workers' Union had advocated) and many women workers are so badly paid that it would take a
lot more than £6 to raise their income to £30 per week. In short,
the TUC were not prepared to fight for a national minimum wage
because it would have involved fighting the government's wage limits.
On abortion, the same conference which rejected the Working Women's
Charter accepted a motion on abortion which called for support for
'free abortion on request'.

5 THE WORKING WOMEN'S CHARTER CAMPAIGN IN NEWCASTLE

The Working Women's Charter group in Newcastle started to organise
in autumn 1974. They produced a videofilm about the Working Women's
Charter using videotape equipment lent by the local Community Development Project. The videofilm, which ran for about twenty minutes,
showed women talking about unions, nurseries, social security,

maternity allowance, abortion and contraception. The film runs
through the points in the Charter, one by one, giving examples of
the way women are exploited both at work and at home and suggesting
ways in which this exploitation may be overcome. We showed the film
to over twenty union branches, tenants' groups and womens' groups
and used it as a basis for discussion around the Working Women's
Charter. We also used it to mobilise support for the conference on
the Working Women's Charter which Newcastle Trades Council held on
12 April. The group was by this time a subgroup of the Trades
Council, and had requested the Trades Council to sponsor the conference.

The Charter Conference in Newcastle was attended by over 100
people. In the morning there were several speakers on women's
position in trade unions, nurseries, and abortion and contraception.
They included the only woman convenor in the north-east in the
engineering industry, who spoke about equal pay, equal opportunity
of entry and promotion, and working conditions. The engineering
industry, she said, now contains as many women as men, and equal pay
is the rule rather than the exception; yet, as in most unions, women
are unwilling to become shop stewards or even to become involved in
the struggle for better pay and conditions. Another speaker, a
housewife and mother, talking of nurseries, pointed out that Newcastle had only 200 nursery places for 5,000 children under five, and
that England compared badly with other European countries in the
provision of nursery facilities. The German Democratic Republic,
for example, provided nurseries for 80 per cent of under-fives. The
Charter, she suggested, demands more nurseries but these must be of
the right kind; for example, they should be provided by councils
wherever possible so that employers cannot exploit women by providing nurseries and holding down wages in return.

The final speaker was a National Union of Public Employees convenor from a Tyneside Hospital who spoke on the need for women to
organise (point 10). Women domestics in her hospital were being
trodden on by the hospital authorities; not only were wages extremely low but they were having to use their own personal cleaning
equipment. The convenor took the lead in organising 180 across
union boundaries, and although the management took no notice at
first, they soon sat up when the women went out on strike. The
strike started at 10 a.m. and by 10.30 the management had offered
£58,000 for more cleaners and equipment - a victory on the women's
part and an example of what can be done through organisation.

In the afternoon there were four workshops, on abortion and
contraception, women in the unions, equal educational and job
opportunities and nurseries. The workshops brought resolutions for
practical activity back to the final plenary session. From the workshop on abortion and contraception, the Tyneside National Abortion
Campaign was set up to campaign against the James White Abortion
(Amendment) Bill. The conference also passed a resolution supporting the formation of women's caucuses in unions, so that women can
organise to oppose discrimination in the unions and at work. There
was a successful creche at the conference staffed by men from
several left-wing groups.

The first main campaign the Charter group became involved in was
the abortion campaign. This was an essential priority in a

situation where the Abortion (Amendment) Bill threatened to restrict severely the availability of abortion and to produce a massive return to back-street abortions. On 7 June there was a local
demonstration of about 100 people in Newcastle against the White
Bill, followed by a public meeting.

ABORTION

'Labour must take a stand, free abortion on demand', and 'Women
must decide their fate, Not the church and not the State'
chanted 100 women and men, marching through Newcastle on Saturday, 7th June to protest against proposed anti-abortion legislation. The demonstration was followed by a public meeting
addressed by Toni Gorton of the National Abortion Campaign and
Dr. Klaus Bergmann, a psychiatrist from Newcastle General Hospital. Dr. Bergmann spoke about the situation before the 1967
Abortion Act, when patients and doctors had to pretend the patient
was near a nervous breakdown or suicide in order to carry out an
abortion. Toni Gorton explained the implications of the White
Bill and how the National Abortion campaign was organising against
it. The chairwoman, Penny Remfry of the Coast Women's Group,
announced further activities of the Tyneside Abortion Campaign.
These include the largest possible mobilisation for the National
Abortion Campaign demonstration on 21st June in London and an
open letter against the White Bill for doctors and other health
workers in this region to sign.
(Extract from 'Workers' Chronicle', published by Newcastle upon
Tyne Trades Council)

Supporters of the Tyneside National Abortion Campaign also took
part in the National Abortion Campaign demonstration in London on 21
June. Newcastle Trades Council passed a resolution opposing the
White Amendment and donated £25 towards the cost of a coach to
London for the demonstration.

The Charter group also worked to publicise the Charter widely.
A four-page bulletin on it was produced by the 'Workers' Chronicle',
and were distributed at several places where women worked. Several
reprints of the bulletin have been produced and sold. The Charter
group has also worked on a series of educational programmes for
Newcastle Radio on the Working Women's Charter and produced an
Access programme for local television. An exhibition on the
Working Women's Charter was organised at Benwell Library and for the
'West End' festival. The exhibition was displayed widely in
colleges, public libraries, community halls and shopping centres.

Newcastle Working Women's Charter group felt that the unionisa-
tion campaign was particularly important in a period of cutbacks and
unemployment when most struggles workers were engaged in tended to
be defensive. In this context, involving women workers who have
traditionally been weakly organised is particularly important. And
as women are the people most affected by cutbacks in social expenditure, it is particularly important that women should be involved and
play a leading role in struggles around the cuts. In late 1975/
early 1976 various organisations, many of them trade-union sponsored,
were set up to oppose cutbacks and unemployment. In Newcastle after

a Trades Council conference in November 1975 a Right to Work
Committee and Tyneside Action Committee against the Cuts were set
up. Members of Newcastle Working Women's Charter group participated in both these. We felt it important to explain that the
slogan of the Right to Work included the right of women to work.
In the case of Tyneside Action Committee against the Cuts, its
first initiative was to support a local demonstration for more
nursery provision on 3 February 1976. The London Working Women's
Charter Co-ordinating Committee held a conference on Women and the
Cuts on 28 February 1976. These initiatives link the Working
Women's Charter Campaign with the campaign against the cuts, and
highlight the need for action against the cuts to take up some of
the demands of Women's Liberation. This is important in developing a real fight against the cuts which can unite all those affected
by them. This direction to the Charter Campaign is also essential
if it is to be involved in the central struggles taking place.

The experiences of the Working Women's Charter Campaign show that
it has been difficult for some Charter groups to make the necessary
contacts with working women. Many groups, including the Newcastle
group, are composed of a few predominantly white-collar women
workers. It is obviously difficult for many women to involve themselves on a long-term basis in the work of the Charter Campaign
because of home commitments (i.e. precisely the problems which give
rise to the need for a Working Women's Charter). Charter groups
can, however, involve wider layers beyond their immediate membership, if they can relate to ongoing activities.

Charter groups need a balance of activity between general publicity around the Working Women's Charter and campaigns. If the
group becomes restricted to publicity, leaflets, speaking at meetings, etc. then it can become marginalised. If the Charter group
takes on a campaign to the exclusion of other activity, the Charter
becomes submerged in that one campaign. This contradicts the essential idea of the campaign, namely that women's problems cannot be
solved by removing one aspect of oppression. This type of publicity
work, using the exhibition and productions of a Charter bulletin,
became an ongoing part of the work of Newcastle Working Women's
Charter Group. In the early part of 1976 they launched a unionisa-
tion campaign around four points.

1 Campaigning for women not in unions to join unions and become
active in them

2 Campaigning for women already in unions to become actively
involved in union affairs.

3 Campaigning for nurseries so that women who want to work and
join unions can do so.

4 Campaigning to change the attitudes of male trade unionists.
The purpose of this campaign was to provide a centralising focus for
activities. It was sponsored by Newcastle Trades Council and
several trade union branches.

The wider long-term aim of such campaigns is to relate ongoing
organisational work around the Charter to specific local campaigns
and issues. The ability to link the Charter campaign into particular
local events is important for winning victories for its demands and
gaining the necessary support to develop it.

THE FUTURE OF THE WORKING WOMEN'S CHARTER CAMPAIGN

The future perspectives cannot be analysed in terms only of the
internal dynamics of the campaign. On the contrary, the purpose
of the Working Women's Charter Campaign is that women and women's
issues play a larger part in the trade union movement and the life
of the working class. Consequently its developments relate to
other developments of the class struggle, particularly over
unemployment, wage limits and cuts in public expenditure. Future
developments are not easily predictable. We can say, however, that
if mass struggles take place around these issues then the Working
Women's Charter Campaign will have a major role in making all
workers in these struggles conscious of the importance these issues
have for women. If these struggles develop, they will also pose
within the workers' movement the need to develop class struggle
for a revolutionary tendency within the trade unions and the
Labour Party to organise the rank and file to fight against the
bureaucracy. Working Women's Charter groups and women's caucuses
in unions are organisations which could be important components of
such a left-wing form of class struggle. Previous rank and file
movements in Britain, such as the Minority Movement in the 1920s,
did not have any demands in their programme relating to women
workers or take up the question of Women's Liberation specifically.
Hopefully we have already achieved enough via the Women's Liberation
Movement and the Working Women's Charter Campaign to ensure that
this is unlikely to happen again. If the struggle for Women's
Liberation is to be taken up as an integral part of the struggle
for socialism, then the Working Women's Charter Campaign has a
crucial role to play in organising towards this objective now.

THE WORKING WOMEN'S CHARTER

We pledge ourselves to organise and agitate to achieve the following
aims:
1 The rate for the job, regardless of sex, at rates negotiated by
   the unions, with a minimum national wage below which no wages
   should fall.
2 Equal opportunity of entry into occupations and in promotion,
   regardless of sex and marital status.
3 Equal education and training for all occupations and compulsory
   day-release for all 16- to 19-year-olds in employment.
4 Working conditions to be, without deterioration of previous
   conditions, the same for women as for men.
5 The removal of all legal and bureaucratic impediments to
   equality, e.g. with regard to tenancies, mortgages, pension
   schemes, taxation, passports, control over children, social
   security payments, hire-purchase agreements, etc.
6 Improved provision of local authority day nurseries, free of
   charge, with extended hours to suit working mothers. Provision
   of nursery classes in day nurseries. More nursery schools.
7 18 weeks' maternity leave with full nett pay before and after the
   birth of a live child; 7 weeks after birth if the child is still-
   born. No dismissal during pregnancy or maternity leave. No
   loss of security, pension or promotion prospects.

8 Family planning clinics supplying free contraception to be
   extended to cover every locality. Free abortion to be readily
   available.
9 Family allowances to be increased to £2.50 per child,
   including the first child.
10 To campaign amongst women to take an active part in the trade
   unions and in political life so that they may exercise influence commensurate with their numbers and to campaign amongst
   male trade unionists that they may work to achieve this aim.

Further reading

COULSON, M., MAGAS, B. and WAINWRIGHT, H., The housewife and her
labour under capitalism: a critique, 'New Left Review', no. 89.
GARDINER, J., Women's domestic labour, 'New Left Review', no. 89.
GARDINER, J., Women and unemployment, 'Red Rag', no. 11.
LLOYD, L., 'Women Workers in Britain', Socialist Woman Publications.
MANDEL, E., 'Bureaucracy', Red Pamphlet no. 5 (from 182 Pentonville
Road, London N1).
MANDEL, E., 'Introduction to Marxist Economic Theory', London, Path-
finder Press.
SECOMBE, W., The housewife and her labour under capitalism, 'New
Left Review', no. 83.
SECOMBE, W., Domestic Labour: a reply, 'New Left Review', no. 94.
WILSON, E., 'Women and the Welfare State', 'Red Rag' pamphlet no. 2,
1974.

3   A local abortion campaign

Two women from the Islington group
of the National Abortion Campaign

This is an account of the activities of one local National Abortion
Campaign (NAC) group, in Islington, north London. Many of our
experiences must have been repeated up and down the country. We
feel they could be of interest to community workers as an example of
highly political agitation in the community, and as a campaign that
particularly involved women.

The national NAC campaign arose as a direct reaction to the threat
of the James White Abortion Amendment Bill presented to Parliament
in February 1975. White sought (and still seeks) to get the 1967
Abortion Act amended in the direction of restriction, on the basis
of claims that the 1967 Act gave 'abortion on demand'. This is not
so, since under this Act abortion is still defined as a crime in all
circumstances except where the dangers to the mental or physical
health of the mother would be greater if her pregnancy went to term
than if her pregnancy were to be terminated, or if there is a danger
to the physical or mental health of the baby. Doctors have leeway
to interpret this in a liberal sense because statistically an abortion before twelve weeks is always safer than pregnancy; this is
really the basis of the so-called 'social clause'. The doctor still
decides, however. The introduction of the James White Bill, therefore, was not to stem a flood of abortion on demand, but had as its
motor power a definitely anti-abortion position. The immediate
excuse for the presentation of the Bill was the now discredited book
'Babies for Burning' which was used as part of a campaign to persuade
MPs and other influential individuals in the community that horrific
abuses were occurring in private clinics offering abortion services
to women who had been unable to get a termination on the National
Health Service. There were allegations both of women being exploited
(e.g. being given an 'abortion' when not pregnant) and of the impro-
per use of foetal material; the Bill was presented to the House of
Commons on the pretence that it was simply tidying up these abuses.
In fact it also sought to introduce restrictions in the availability
of abortion and to make the giving of advice and information about
abortion illegal. It ignored the Report of the Lane Commission,
which has bever been debated in Parliament but which had broadly supported the 1967 Abortion Act, and was in effect an attempt to undo
that Act and to return to the situation as it existed before 1967,

or worse. It is important too to be aware that the White Bill was the outcome of years of campaigning by SPUC (the Society for the Protection of the Unborn Child) and that the SPUC campaign against abortion is in itself an all too successful example of grass-roots and national campaigning at every level, backed by an experienced and extremely powerful pressure group - the Roman Catholic church.

One of the demands of the Women's Liberation Movement is for free contraception and abortion on demand, and prior to the James White Bill, the Women's Abortion and Contraception Campaign had been in operation for several years. Its activities had been sporadic, but although it had never really got off the ground at a national level in some areas it was very successful. For instance in Bristol the WACC group has been running a pregnancy testing service for over two years and has drawn into its orbit as helpers, volunteers and campaigners a number of the women who came in the first place just for the test. It has been concerned with campaigning for NHS facilities for abortion in the Bristol area, and for contraceptive facilities, and has done much propaganda work to put forward progressive ideas on fertility control, emphasising the importance of a woman's right to choose when she will become pregnant - her right to have children - as well as the right to abortion, and combating ideas of population control and manipulation by the state.

The threat of restrictive legislation mobilised the women's movement into concerted nationwide activity. The National Abortion Campaign, set up in February 1975, represented the joint forces of feminists, political groups and pressure groups that had long been fighting on the single issue of the liberalisation of the abortion laws.

Throughout the spring and summer of 1975 our local campaign group met every Friday in the early evening. Usually there were between thirty and forty of us from different parts of Islington. We represented different sections of the Islington community, although women committed to feminism predominated. Most of us came from women's groups, from squatting groups, from the Communist Party and International Marxist Group, from the Labour Party and from the Islington Trades Council, Islington Community Law Centre and the Essex Road Women's Centre. This Centre provided a useful focus for the campaign. We met there each week; it was known in the area and many women from local estates as well as from activist groups turned up, so it was a good place from which to publicise the campaign against the Bill.

Our local NAC campaign differed from the generality of local campaigns in being organised around a national issue. It was more like a local than a national campaign on the other hand, in that it represented an immediate gut reaction to a distinct and urgent threat. Yet although similar to campaigns against, for example, the building of a motorway or the demolition of housing, it was a defensive campaign (in this case the defence of the only mildly liberal 1967 Abortion Act), like such campaigns, too, it at once went on the offensive for a woman's right to choose and free abortion on demand. We had two definite foci of activity, shared with groups throughout the country. The first was petition-collecting and the second was to build our strength and gain publicity for the National Abortion Demonstration on Saturday 21 June.

It was a fine hot summer and the weather helped to give us even
more enthusiasm and success. We collected signatures on petitions
each Saturday in the main Islington market, Chapel Market, and at
the Nag's Head, Holloway, the other busy shopping centre. We also
went in twos and threes to tube stations throughout the borough to
catch people coming home from work in the late afternoons. Getting
the petitions signed was a surprisingly easy task. We had antici-
pated at least some hostility because abortion is supposed to be a
controversial issue. On the contrary, while we encountered ignorance of the whole issue - the majority of those approached had not
even heard of James White or the threat to abortion rights - we met
with refusal from very few individuals. The petitions became an
opportunity to inform and educate the local public about the situation and thus performed a vital purpose. The most prominent reaction among people approached was to agree that abortion should be
the right of the woman to choose - not doctors, priests or anyone
else - but it was especially noticeable that the immediate response
of working-class women was usually something on the lines of 'if
this happens it will be the back-street abortionists again'. This
was particularly true of older women and no doubt reflected the
experience of their lives. Most striking was the immediate recognition of the importance of the abortion issue to women. This was
also the case with working-class men. Middle-class men, on the
other hand, the group least likely to sign, in some cases took up a
lofty and patronising attitude, and some of them said they felt the
issue had nothing to do with men at all!

Another area of activity was to try to alert local individuals,
such as general practitioners, to the danger presented by the White
Bill, and to find out which GPs were sympathetic on the issue. The
most helpful doctor we encountered was a woman gynaecologist. She
spoke at the local public meeting we held to publicise the campaign
further, along with other local women, a councillor, lawyers and
health workers. At this meeting there was also a Street Theatre
satire on the White Bill and SPUC campaign, which related the issue
of abortion to women's position more generally.

Our campaign enabled us to publicise the lack of abortion facilities in the Islington area. We had already lost the Liverpool Road
branch of the Royal Free Hospital - which had dealt with maternity
and gynaecological cases, including terminations - and we were able
to combine with local groups who had been active on this issue and
extend our work to cover the Whittington Hospital and Royal Northern
Hospital as well, where we feared that abortion facilities might also
be under attack. There were thus ample opportunities in Islington
to make the vital link between abortion as a women's issue and abortion as one aspect of the attack on the NHS, and we linked this even
further with the whole general issue of social welfare cuts.
Finally, some of us who are on the Islington Trades Council saw that
the issue was raised and debated there, and the Trades Council passed
a resolution opposing the proposed legislation and later brought its
banner to the national demonstration.

The bulk of these activities were directed either at politically
active individuals, whether in the labour movement or in the local
community, or at specially interested groups, such as GPs and
health workers. We found, however, that although housewives were

unlikely to come regularly to the meetings, some of those we knew
were very eager to take the petitions round their estates, so that
there were really two levels of activity going on all the time, and
the issue must have been very widely discussed throughout the
borough.

All this led up to the national demonstration on 21 June. We
had discussed the possibility of having a float, but in the end
decided to make singing our particular activity. We had several
rehearsals beforehand and members of the group prepared song-
sheets for distribution on the march - familiar folk songs with
specially written words. On the march itself we had a very large if
somewhat rambling contingent and most of us marched behind the
Essex Road Women's Centre banner. The rally at Hyde Park must have
been attended by between 25,000 and 30,000 people and was an
impressive culmination of the work we had done alongside all the
other NAC groups.

That was really the end of the campaign for the summer. In the
autumn, after the automatic fall of the White Bill with the ending
of the Parliamentary session, the orientation of the campaign became
rather confused. A Select Committee had been set up to examine the
Bill and had already reported on abuses in the private sector (its
recommendations have already been put into effect by the undemo-
cratic means of a DHSS circular). It was known that this Select
Committee was likely to be reconvened, but repeated delays and the
procedural complexity of the issue made it a difficult focus around
which to organise. Some labour movement activists were reluctant to
campaign against restrictions in the private sector when they were
opposed (as we were too) to the very existence of a private sector.
A very large national conference held by NAC in October attended by
nearly 1,000, mostly women, was a rather dispiriting event for many
and, while it showed the degree of concern the whole issue had
aroused, did not succeed in focusing the campaign, being marred by
sectarianism.

A few of us in Islington - about ten - continued co meet through
the autumn, but as our numbers were now small we were unable to
engage in any very spectacular activity to mark the Week of Action
called by NAC in November. We had a local march and sing-song with
leaflets round the markets near the Angel on the Saturday morning of
the national rally in Trafalgar Square, and some of us attended the
mass lobby of MPs at the House of Commons.

This was really intended as a mass demonstration as much as an
opportunity to speak with MPs, and as such was not a great success.
Our main impression was of the hostility expressed, even by those
MPs who claimed to be ultra-sympathetic on the issue, towards the
campaign. It is fair to say that some of this antagonism seemed
rather to be directed towards Women's Liberation in general, and
would probably have been found in any male grouping of a similar
class and age. Many older women were present, yet we were all
addressed by most of the MPs as if we were hysterical young girls.
It was instructive to compare this event, which really fell between
two stools, with our experience of lobbying one of our local MPs
just before Christmas. This was a joint delegation with members of
the Trades Council, and the local Labour Party was also represented,
and it was a helpful discussion in which a number of issues were

aired and misunderstandings cleared up. For example we explained that the slogan 'Abortion on Demand' did not necessarily imply that we supported abortion in the eighth month of pregnancy. Our MP evidently understood our position better by the end of the meeting and had been able to assure himself that we had considered the issue seriously. It seems that this discussion was one factor in changing his position on the question of the reconvening of the Select Committee. Although a supporter of the 1967 Act, he had shared the view of a number of pro-abortion MPs that the Select Committee could serve a useful purpose in looking more widely at the whole issue of abortion. We disputed this view, not least because of the composition of the Committee, since a majority of the MPs serving on it were known anti-abortionists - that is, they were opposed to abortion on principle, rather than being concerned simply with possible abuses of the Act. Our contact with our MP was a political lesson in the right and wrong way of approaching this aspect of our work. It is quite clear that the flood of letters from SPUC supporters and Roman Catholic congregations to the MPs has impressed those MPs and that as a consequence they have lost touch with the real feeling of the majority of individuals in this country (opinion polls have shown a majority in favour even of abortion on demand). Therefore both the mass campaign and the parliamentary campaign are very important. (Indeed it would be wrong to separate them.)

One interesting point raised by our MP was the general dearth of information on the variability of NHS facilities for abortion, including day-care abortion, throughout the country, and he suggested that it would be worth while for the national campaign to collect such information in a systematic way for presentation to the government. This relates to our own local activities in trying to clarify the position in Islington, and indeed probably our most useful activity in the autumn was to make links with the Community Health Council in order further to investigate the situation with regard to the NHS in Islington. Some of us visited local hospitals and talked to consultants.

At the time of writing (April 1976), our struggle, locally and nationally, is still far from over. The Select Committee has been reconvened, and the MPs sympathetic to abortion have resigned from it in protest, so that it now has manifestly an anti-abortion focus. Pro-abortion groups, such as NAC, who have refused to appear before it may be compelled to do so. It is hoped to set up an alternative tribunal as a counter-focus, and local groups will collect information on the reality of abortion facilities in their areas.

Our local campaign is more lively than it was in the autumn. We recently held a fund-raising benefit for the national campaign, and once again formed a large contingent for the 3 April march and rally. In general we have continued to centre our activities on local issues, making provision of an out-patient abortion clinic our main priority. We have held a meeting for health workers on this issue in one of the local hospitals, but we are working mainly through the Community Health Council at the moment. This meeting was in fact not particularly well attended and made us realise that the issue is one which still needs much discussion at many different levels. While there clearly is mass support for liberal abortion

laws, the problem as usual remains how to mobilise this support
over a long period. Nor is it always easy to relate the abortion
issue to the wider issue of the position of women, or the right to
sexual pleasure. To widen our agitational work we are putting
together a display on abortion and are hoping to go into schools to
discuss it with teenagers, hoping that this will place abortion in a
more rational perspective in the light of contraceptive failure and
drawbacks and women's need to be able to plan their pregnancies.

    In all this, we have learned much about political organising,
how to connect with local women and with public bodies, and have
found out much about our own locality. The immediate gut-reaction
phase of the NAC campaign is well and truly over now, and we, like
groups all over the country, have to take breath and organise ourselves for the long haul that lies ahead.

4   A lesson in day care

Valerie Charlton

The Children's Community Centre at 123 Dartmouth Park Hill, London
N19, is more specifically a full-time parent-controlled nursery for
children from 2½ to 5 years. It is partially financed by a local
council grant and is staffed by two full-time workers and a rota
of voluntary labour, usually parents.

It took almost two years to set up and was opened in December
1972, so at the time of writing (November 1975) it is entering its
fourth year of existence. What I hope to do in this article is to
describe how the centre was initially a product of prevailing ideas
and circumstances and how those ideas were changed through being put
into practice. Since December 1972, each year at the centre has
been dominated by different problems, or more accurately the same
range of problems but with a changing emphasis. The minor irrita-
tions of one year would become the insoluble contradictions of the
next. Those of us involved had our political consciousness forcibly
raised by seeing ideas we had cherished producing contradictions we
could not solve. Which means that some of us now want nurseries that
would be quite different in many ways from the Children's Community
Centre (CCC). This is to emphasise, not minimise, the importance of
that experience but also to recognise another contradiction.
Although individuals have grown and developed through their experience at the Centre, the Centre itself does not, I believe, have that
capacity.

However, to begin at the beginning. The idea for the CCC grew in
the very first place out of discussions among a group of women
representatives of the twelve or so Women's Liberation Groups in
Camden in 1970. The local council had shown an interest in our ideas
and we decided to take them up on this. That group dwindled over a
period of weeks leaving three of us to develop the scheme. We were
joined after a while by four local women, and the seven of us, all
with children under five, formed a stable group which worked for
twenty months negotiating before the nursery opened.

Many influences determined the form of the CCC. In the first
place, if we had asked for a brand new purpose-built council nursery
none of our children would have been eligible for places in it. Nor
could we have had any control over how it was run or what its principles were, aside from the problem of being powerless to persuade

31

the council to spend that sort of money. So our first necessity
was that we should have control.

Our experience in the Women's Liberation Movement was the most
powerful influence. One of the original demands of the WLM was
for free 24-hour nurseries for all under-fives. Though it sounds
simple enough it was confusing and unworkable, The 24-hour aspect
frightened people who took it to mean that the same children stayed
there for 24 hours a day instead of recognising it as provision for
the children of women night-workers such as cleaners and nurses.
But more important it did not ask for a qualitative change in the
nursery system, mainly because at that time the movement was divided
about the sort of changes it wanted and there were no models to
refer to. Many women thought the dismal state of nursery provision
was because it was state controlled, the 'alternative' being community control. We were to learn that the two are not mutually exclu-
sive and that community control holds as many contradictions as
state control when each is seen in isolation.

Coming from the WLM the demand did have an implicit and crucial
emphasis which was absent from all other nursery demands of the
time. We wanted nurseries which acknowledged and catered for the
needs of women as well as the needs of children, but confusion arose
from the neglect to make this explicit in the demand. We were committed to the needs of women while demanding more of something which
blatantly ignored these needs. The existing nursery system does
that, then and now, not only by lack of provision but by dividing
the provision so that no one part of it satisfies all women's needs.
For example, day nurseries are the only ones open long enough to be
of use to women in full-time employment, but they usually provide
only enough places for what they call 'priority cases'; i.e. children of single parents or the 'underprivileged', and they thereby
connect full-time day care with deprivation, a stigma which has yet
to be overcome. Day nurseries are run by the Department of Health
and Social Security and charges are made according to a means test.
They take children aged from six weeks to five years and have an
emphasis on health care rather than education. They are headed by
matrons and staffed by nursery nurses, the lowest paid of nursery
workers, and are renowned for their rigidity (although we are hearing of a growing number of exceptions). Most working women have
therefore to find a private solution in using child-minders, where
there is no control on charges, quality of care or education.
Child-minders are nevertheless the most commonly used form of child
care.

Nursery schools, playgroups and creches provide only morning or
afternoon sessions of school hours or less. Nursery schools are run
by Education Departments, staffed by teachers and (oddly enough) are
interested in education but take children only over the age of
three. Playgroups also take only three- to five-year-olds, but are
grant aided and depend on voluntary labour of 'mothers'. This is
made possible by a training course, allowing some women an area of
expansion, albeit within limited definitions, which enables them to
go on and qualify for teaching careers. But essentially playgroups
support and encourage women's role in the family by showing 'women'
how to cope more effectively with the socialisation and education of
their children.

In constructing the principles of the CCC, we were attempting, among many other things, to discover a model for a better nursery demand for the women's movement. We wanted to bring together the best aspects of what existed - long hours of care to meet the needs of working women, better care and education and also create the possibility of exploring two main themes. These were to challenge sex roles among ourselves and the children and secondly to develop collective, non-authoritarian ways of organising and learning.

There were other valuable considerations particular to our group. For example, six out of the seven had had experience in teaching, and this became an asset to the centre and added to our confidence. It was also a point carefully noted by council officers when they came to look us over (six teachers for free in one nursery!). Some of us were particularly good at dealing with council red tape, and we had a general political perspective. But, most important, because our paid work was limited through having young kids, we all had time, not to mention staying power.

For twenty months we sat them out, harassing the council at intervals, asking for commitments, and not allowing them to forget us. Finally, when we decided we had waited long enough, we threatened them with exposure in the newspapers. That did the trick and we were eventually given a renovated short-life house in a redevelopment area. Although the council had been incredibly slow, they had never resisted our demands and were in fact suspiciously enthusiastic. They gave us an annual grant based on their costing which, if anything, was more that we would have asked for. (That is no longer the case, however.)

In our eagerness to get into the house, we made one very naive and stupid mistake. We offered to decorate the whole house ourselves, hoping to involve local people at this stage. This was a catastrophe. Of course no local people wanted to come and paint a house for people they didn't know, so about half our number (the other half being otherwise occupied - for which they have not, to this day, been forgiven) did a complete decorating job which took weeks because the builders left all sorts of other jobs to be included in the decorating.

THE FIRST YEAR

We selected our full-time worker and in early December 1972 opened the Centre with a huge sigh of relief. The first year was amazing. We quickly manipulated our grant to allow also for a paid part-time worker and these two women made the Centre come to life. Their energy, initiative and organising ability came at exactly the right time when the original group were exhausted and demoralised by the long wait. However, seeing the place in action gradually re-enthused us and we involved ourselves in the detail of organisation. Collective organising in this situation was a practical necessity as well as an ideal. We, the original organisers, the paid workers and new parents were collectively responsible for the success and running of the Centre. A situation had to be established where all had equal rights and took responsibility by choice, not by force of authority.

We were all expected to attend a weekly Sunday night meeting.
Here we organised the weekly rota and sorted out who would cook
lunches, do shopping, go to the laundrette or take the kids out.
Later we managed to pay a nominal sum to a woman who came regularly
to cook lunches. We had a treasurer who kept accounts and to whom
we also paid a small sum, and we did pay full rates for a woman to
clean each evening, but we all helped with things like paying bills,
ordering stock and getting repairs done to the house. Where possible we encouraged men to work on the rota and do their share of
all other tasks.

A large part of every meeting was spent discussing a theme around
which to build the children's activities of the week. This formed a
link between the workers on different days and could help when
people were short of ideas. It meant that what one did with the
children was not a completely individual responsibility. The previous week's theme would be reported on so that we could see the
success or failure of the various ideas.

Having planned the week ahead and distributed jobs, we tried to
talk about two children per week with their parents present. Pre-
dictably parents had a compelling interest in knowing how their child
was getting on and could voice anxieties or enlighten us as to what
was happening to the child at home.

> Not as it were to a group of professionals but to a group made up
> largely of other parents who know their children and work with
> them ... so discussion is based not on asking the advice of
> experts but on the exchange of experience and common ideas.
> (From Not so much a Day Nursery, 'Spare Rib', no. 17)

Or at least that's what we wanted it to be! Whether that was the
real situation is another story, but if it was not, we certainly
were not aware of it that first year.

The meetings were quite well attended but always by the same
people, basically those who worked on the rota. Try as we did we
could not involve the others. This was a source of irritation
because their children were the ones who were at the centre for the
longest hours precisely because the parents were in full-time
employment. There was the odd moan on this point from time to time
but this was generally overcome by the feeling that those who worked
on the rota were able to do so because they were more privileged
and/or middle class. (Later on we had to distinguish more carefully
between these two categories.)

We kept a daily journal where the progress and problems of each
day were recorded. Each person who worked at the centre was expected
to read it and write in it - and still is. It provided a link between people who never crossed paths except at the Sunday meeting and
was often a tactful way of making criticisms. The need to report on
a day's work helped to get things in order and made us consider more
carefully what was happening. It also gave us a permanent and ongoing record of changes and developments since we began.

It was very important to some of us that our children should not
suffer the same restrictions as a result of their sex as we had done.
So we tried to encourage the girls to be less afraid and fight back
if attacked and the boys to be more gentle and caring. At the age
of three, there were quite well established general differences between the two sexes.

> All activities are made available for children of both sexes
> but it's not enough simply to treat all children equally. The
> boys have frequently already learned their advantage and are
> quick to make capital out of it. There has to be positive
> support in favour of the girls who are generally already less
> adventurous. (From 'The Patter of Tiny Contradictions', Red
> Rag pamphlet no. 5)

We encouraged boys to do traditionally female activities such as
cooking and shopping, and the girls to use hammers and saws. The
children got used to seeing men cooking the lunch and women changing plugs or putting up shelves. (It seems almost ludicrous now
that a sexual demarcation line could have existed which prevented
women 'changing plugs' - even to the extent that women could actually have believed themselves to be incapable of doing it.)

Self-sufficiency among the children was an important aim. They
were found to be capable of far more than even - or especially -
their parents believed. It was eye-opening to see how as a mother
one had become used to doing things for children automatically, even
when this was quite unnecessary and in fact debilitating to the
child. It took a critical collective situation to expose this.
If the children were really in difficulties we encouraged them to
seek the help of their peers first, in the hope that this would
develop consideration and sensitivity towards each other, and I
think we had some success.

Throughout, with the children as with the adults, there was that
tension between sensitivity to need and the challenge of passivity
and dependence. We flipped from side to side, sometimes over-
emphasising the one and forgetting the other and then compensating.
It was often quite agonising and we all suffered from time to time.
But to have to examine one's ideas and one's practice was a positive
product of collective organising. It also meant a sharing of skills
and knowledge and a renewing of initiative which had often been
stifled by perpetually accepting instructions in all sorts of
authoritarian situations, i.e. school, work, family.

We realised early in that first year that if we were to function
properly we had to be extremely well organised. People were expected
to be responsible and reliable and generally they were. The atmosphere was alive and positive (that is if you happened to be one of
the vocal, involved people), and we all felt some pride in what we
had achieved. A further, most important, not-to-be-forgotten source
of elation, which we all shared, was a change in our material circumstances because our children were in a nursery; suddenly all sorts
of things were possible: we felt human again.

In the spring we had one of the best public meetings I have been
to, where we each took turns in describing different aspects of how
the Centre functioned. We made huge charts as visual aids which
showed how we organised ourselves, where to get cheap furniture and
equipment, the structure of the local council and which parts were
penetrable, and many other useful tips on how to start your own
neighbourhood nursery. At the meeting many people spoke publicly for
the first time and felt very pleased with themselves. We thought we
had hit on such a good idea that we wanted as many people as possible
to start their own centres and thereby have some effect on the overall shortage of nurseries. Later we had a press conference, gave

many individual interviews to newspapers and magazines, even gave a
couple of radio interviews. We had already published a pamphlet
describing setting up the Centre. We talked of making a film and
we offered to speak to any group interested. We were inundated with
visitors. Publicity was an essential part of our work if we were
to be the first of many children's community centres.

By that summer we were aware of a few problems. Some parents who
worked at the Centre, especially but not exclusively those without
teaching experience, felt and were ill equipped to cope with the
work. It had been naive of us to expect anything different. We
realised that we had to set aside time where adults could help each
other to learn how to work with the children and to discuss both the
ideological and the practical content of what we call 'education'.
(The Play Groups Association had been quick to recognise that the
use of voluntary labour can work only with the support of a training
course.)

We felt a vague unease about the use of 'voluntary labour', but
thought we would be able gradually to pay more people from what we
blithely thought would be an increasing council grant. The unease
was also offset by the sense that we were using the situation to try
out some very important ideals, even if we had very little choice
anyway.

We recognised that we should start negotiating for another property (our expected life-span in that building was three years),
given the time it had taken to get this one. We saw the new one as
having to include facilities for under-twos and a women's centre -
a daytime place where women could meet and get away from their kids
with the possibility of overnight stay. We had more than once had
to let women use the Centre as a refuge from a tyrannical husband
or unbearable situation at home.

At one point that summer we became aware that we were not too
popular in the neighbourhood, and this thoroughly shocked us. Why
should we be disliked, as we were providing an important service,
largely at our own cost, and we were very nice people? Two of us
volunteered to attend a local tenants' meeting to 'explain' what we
were about. We were doubly shocked at the venomous treatment we
received. Resentment was felt on several counts by older residents.
First of all our nursery was free and the local day nursery which
their children had attended was not. We were being funded by a council grant which came out of their rates. What's more we were middle
class! hippies! and they didn't want our type invading their
already disrupted neighbourhood (the fact that we all lived permanently within a mile's radius at the most was ignored). This was
all quite staggering but made us realise just how redevelopment had
destroyed a very old community and how the bitterness of that was
bound to be directed at relative newcomers like ourselves who by our
use of short-life property were taking advantage of the situation.
The redevelopment had been going on for years, and meanwhile shop-
keepers had been moving out and their shops were becoming derelict.
People who wanted to remain in the area were moved out of their
homes into temporary accommodation, only to see their old houses
squatted by the homeless for very long periods. Council rebuilding
either moved very slowly or not at all, depending on the state of the
finances. It was, however, a very serious problem for us not to have

the support of that tenants' association, and the reluctance of the
council to increase our grant in the following and subsequent years
was certainly affected by this.

THE SECOND YEAR

That first year we had been preoccupied with establishing our organisation. The second year was the test of that organisation.
Relief and enthusiasm had carried us through so far but as each of
us got used to the situation and expanded our work outside, the
demands that the Centre made on us began to be felt as an intrusion,
especially by those who had been involved for almost two years
before it opened. Like any other institution, there would be the
normal amount of absenteeism, people going sick or on holiday, and
whenever this happened we all had to give more time. For example,
when our 'paid' cleaner went on holiday for two or three weeks we
had to take turns in doing two hours' cleaning at the end of every
day. This was very enlightening and made us all be much cleaner
during the day, but it was a strain on everybody. Another even
worse situation was when our full-time worker had a serious road
accident and was away for many weeks. We were all forced to take
on even more responsibility which again increased our collective
sense but drained us in the process.
   It was in this climate that we tried to do two things that year.
First, we had promised to produce a much more comprehensive pamphlet describing the Centre, and second, we started in earnest
trying to determine what sorts of changes would be necessary when
we were rehoused. We were still under the impression that we could
get from the council more or less what we asked for. But the more
we discussed these issues the more confused we became as a group.
We began to split in different directions. Some people became
annoyed about the time spent in arguments about money, principles
and the like, when the important job of working with children was
suffering some neglect. Others felt it was imperative to work out
our politics and be self-critical if necessary. The result was that
it took some eight or nine months to produce our pamphlet.
   The pressure we were under both as individuals and as a group
coloured everything. The irritation which was felt by some against
those people with children at the nursery full time and yet didn't
attend meetings or contribute in any way turned into real resentment,
tinged with envy. These antagonisms would often be expressed as
dislike of someone and interpreted as 'personality problems'. But I
think it is very important to recognise that this was the real
expression of different interests. For example (fortunately for
us), one of the parents who was an object of resentment recognised
the predicament of her group and was courageous enough to spell it
out for us in her contribution to the pamphlet:
   It is easy to see how the centre can appear to an outsider as a
   trendy playgroup, essentially middle class but providing a few
   places for working class children to justify the grant received
   from the council. By choosing to provide a service in Highgate
   New Town and yet to insist on involving parents on a rota system,
   the centre is faced with an insoluble conflict of purpose.

Working class parents, working full time, are unlikely to be able to give any time at all on the rota and it is difficult to feel totally involved and responsible, as the group demands, if one is not concerned in the day to day activities of the children.

The Sunday meetings also expose another area of class difference. Most of the middle class parents are fairly articulate. They are at home with abstract argument, full of jargon and references to authors one may or may not have heard of. It is not surprising that many parents lose heart and seldom come to meetings.

This outraged most people, and one woman responded indignantly, pointing out what it cost her to be involved at the Centre:

I welcomed the concept of parent participation and control, as did my husband, Hugo, who went into part time teaching to make it possible. I teach in the evenings and work half days Saturdays and Sundays to make it economically possible. But because of our commitment to our jobs, the centre and our four children, I have less time to myself as a woman and to explore the work I am committed to as a sculptor than I had two years ago. ...

But the centre has made assumptions about both myself and Hugo that we ourselves have fortified by the nature of our commitment there. The assumption is that we are comfortable, middle class with all the time in the world to help and contribute. Also I feel under pressure because it would not be 'right' under my label of middle class to say I would prefer to use the time at the centre to expand my work - that to help me properly as a working woman I need to give up working on the rota and have a full time place for the youngest child who is still there.

Some of us then saw that in our eagerness to ensure that we catered for a variety of needs we had succeeded in putting two groups of people in a very unpleasant relationship with each other. To put it crudely, the labour of the more middle-class group was being used to subsidise a largely working-class group, who had no real way of being involved, and therefore of contributing, even had they wanted to. It was an essentially patronising situation complicated by the fact that many in that 'middle-class' group were far from privileged and were single parents, struggling with their own lives, in some cases worse off than the working people they were subsidising.

To complicate matters further, we had been refused an increase in our grant that year on the ground that we did not cater for enough children (we took twelve children full time and six part time). The council said that if we needed more money we should charge fees. This was a nonsense to us. We had set up the place, we staffed and administered it with our own valuable labour time and in addition we were being expected to charge ourselves fees. The money we might have raised from parents who did not work on the rota would not anyway have made a substantial difference. Even apart from all this, some of us believed that nurseries should be an extension of general education and should therefore be financed in the same way. Our insistence on 'free' nursery places at our Centre was an important way of raising the argument.

Part of the council's reasoning was that the local day nursery was not filled to capacity, so why should they give increased support to us. They refrained from explaining that the wages of nursery nurses were so low that the day nursery could not get the staff to work there and this was why it was under-subscribed. Meanwhile the Centre had long waiting lists.

It was increasingly clear to us, in spite of our internal conflicts, that the dominant need in that neighbourhood, where there were so many unsupported mothers and families with both parents out at work, was for full-time day care without additional demands on parents. We were able to provide only five places of this sort and we felt obliged to give these places to people whose need was greatest, but when everybody's need is great, selection becomes odious.

Inflation was adding stress to the situation and forcing even more women 'out' to work. The only way we would be able to take more children of working parents would be to employ another full-time paid worker whom we could not afford on our present grant.

Our first year's grant had been £3,000 with an additional once-only payment of £1,500 with which to equip and decorate the place. In 1973-4 we had applied for £4,500 but were given only £4,000. Our application for 1974-5 had to be over £7,000 if we were to employ a second worker; knowing our survival to be dependent on this, we went ahead and advertised for a second worker to start in September 1974. The feeling at the time was that we could 'force' the council to give us the extra money. Admittedly this was naive but we felt we had no choice. Needless to say we did not receive the increase and the problems of our third year were to be defined by this.

During our second year we became aware of yet another problem related to our use of voluntary labour. This year, 1973-4, there had been the beginnings of some organising by other state nursery workers. They began to join trade unions and question both their levels of pay and the differences of pay between them which was the product of different forms of training. Clearly there are many anomalies of pay, qualifications and training, not to mention working conditions, hours worked, holidays, etc., arising from the administrative divisions which I mentioned earlier between day nurseries, nursery schools and playgroups.

Some of us began to see that to press for a growth in the number of our type of nurseries which depended on voluntary 'unqualified' labour would be directly undermining the nursery workers' struggle. Already we had heard of matrons of day nurseries using voluntary labour rather than filling a vacant situation with paid staff.

The danger of our situation was brought home to us in an even more suspicious way when, in our search for larger premises, the possibility was raised of us taking over a large day nursery which provided full-time places for fifty children. We would run the place on a system of voluntary labour, thereby replacing a large percentage of the fifty places with children whose parents could provide voluntary labour. This would have meant that effectively we would have been responsible for reducing the number of full-time state nursery places. We realised how vulnerable our structure was to misuse, especially now that many more nurseries faced cutbacks and closure.

In addition, the 'ideology', as opposed to the actuality, of parent participation and control which governed the Centre had some

pernicious undertones. For some it was a way for mothers to spend
even more time preoccupied with the business of child care, albeit
in a social situation, and occasionally one could detect a moral
self-righteousness directed at women who could not or did not want
to work with small children - we do it because we care more!

There also developed a rather overblown sense of our own importance at the Centre. We did not practice sexist child care like the
state nurseries. We were not authoritarian and rigid like the state
nurseries. We knew more about under-five care and education than
nursery workers who were unaware, poorly educated and definitely
not into alternative politics!

A minority of us at the Centre began to find the elitism quite
offensive and believed that it had a definite class base. After
all, state nurseries were in the main for working-class children
and were staffed in the main by working-class women. This in no way
meant that they were beyond criticism, and changes clearly have to
occur; but the fact is that nursery workers in state nurseries, by
being organised in unions (acknowledging the problems they are having
in even getting into that position), are probably the most crucial
factor in a move towards a better nursery system. Our Centre has
contributed ideas on non-sexist and non-authoritarian child care but
is helpless to change the main material conditions necessary before
our ideas can be put into practice on a large scale. That can be
done, in my opinion, only with the organised agitation and power of
the trade union movement and the women's movement.

THE THIRD YEAR

We faced the third year with our initial confidence badly shaken as
we realised the complexity of our position. Many of the original
people were moving on as their children started school. The rota
was more unreliable than it had ever been. The house was deteriora-
ting and there was no money for repairs. Rehousing seemed unlikely
and, overriding all else, we had not enough money to get through the
year.

We had employed two new full-time workers, who through no fault of
their own inherited a very difficult situation. Morale was very low
and disagreements between people quite severe. Instead of our
earlier waiting lists, we actually had vacancies. I am not quite
sure why that was, except that our area had a constantly changing
population and this seemed to be a time when there were few people
with small children.

We put in an application for Urban Aid, which is a government
grant given with the backing of local councils to 'new' schemes which
are of service to the community. We presented a 'new' project where
we tried to accommodate parent participation in a way that would be
much more reciprocal. The CCC would become a place where parents,
through study, interchange and their own practice, could learn about
under-five care and education. We might be linked with a polytechnic or university and would be able to award qualifications. The
parents/students would be grant aided and this would solve the problem of both staffing the centre and voluntary labour. The Centre
would necessarily be expanded and rehoused to take many more

children. Naturally the possibility of doing such a course would
not be limited just to parents but work with the children
could be confined to those who really wanted to. The discussion
of our application among ourselves caused yet more disagreement as
we were not even united about the nature of the problems. It was,
however, a somewhat desperate, if convoluted, attempt to ensure
the continuance of the Centre while removing some of the anomalies.

We didn't get Urban Aid, and our problems continued.

We had to find ways of economising. We put up the charges for
dinners. We got a little money from charity. After dozens of
letters and much deliberation, the council gave us a subsidiary
grant of £700. They had said glibly, 'Why don't you have jumble
sales?', and we did - until people were sick to death of jumble
sales. Our precious autonomy was in fact the autonomy to raise
around £2,000 a year in order to keep going.

It was clear that this could not go on indefinitely and no group,
however committed, could sustain the effort of raising £40 per week.
What's more, if we proved to the council that we could raise that
amount, then there was little chance of getting our grant increased.
Also we were angry that we had done so much only to find that the
impossible was expected of us. It was infuriating to have to pay so
highly for the care of one's child. We choked every time the
'freeness' of the Centre was referred to.

Our only hope, it seemed, would be to alter our financial relationship with the council. We had relied on an annual grant for
which we had to re-apply each year when we presented our accounts.
Because we put such value on autonomy and parents' control, we were
completely at their mercy, and this made nonsense of our control
and autonomy. Our real relation to the council was exposed, also
our real class relation to one another. The economic instability
began to outweigh the advantages of exploration. We needed the
council to take us over so that we could be properly and permanently
financed.

It is for this reason that I firmly believe that 'alternatives',
particularly in the area of education, can have only a transient
value, however great that may be. By 'alternatives', I mean those
organisations which, because they want to explore different values,
ideals and politics, necessarily have to exist outside, either partially or totally, the state system of financing. I believe there
comes a time when if those values and ideals are important to
everyone they must be fought for within state institutions in order
ultimately to change the nature of the state. We had hoped we could
see this transition through at the Centre - keep our values but
within a properly equipped and fully financed nursery with a fully
paid staff.

This was a subject of many discussions and raised real threats to
some people. Would they still have a place for their child in such
a nursery? How could they afford the fees that could well come with
the package? Would we really be able to keep control? We didn't
know. All we knew was that our system had limitations which were
also beyond us. We presented our newest idea to the council only to
be told, very pleasantly, that if they took us over, as it were, they
would only be giving themselves the problems that we had - rehousing,
need for more money, etc. - and why should they do that?

My picture of this year is limited to one of argument and discussion among the adults. My own child had left after the first year. I continued to work on the rota for the second year but during the third year I went only to meetings. Other people were still very much involved with the children and enjoyed and valued that experience as well as drawing more optimism from it than I personally felt. Nevertheless the year was a difficult one, and when parents left the Centre it was often with relief to be out of something which had grown quite oppressive.

One uplift at the end of that year was the production of a film - '123' - which had been made by one of the parents. This described enthusiastically and very prettily the best aspects of the Centre: the parent involvement and the relaxed and thoughtful attitudes to the children. It rather skimmed over the problems and for this I would criticise it, but the film has had a very wide distribution in colleges and all sorts of groups and never fails, it seems, to raise important discussions, especially when accompanied by a speaker from the Centre. The economic problems, however, are definitive, and to promote the good aspects without being very specific about the shaky structure is very misleading. This film is now being used by the Social Services Department of Camden Council as an example of a 'real' community nursery. This is worrying, unless careful qualifications are made.

In 1974-5 the Centre had expenditure of £7,875 and an income of £6,507. The council grant was £4,800 and the rest was raised in a multitude of ways through the efforts of people at the Centre.

THE FOURTH YEAR

This present year, 1975-6, I can describe only through fairly scanty talks with people who still work at the Centre, as I am no longer personally involved. This year's grant is expected to be cut by 5 per cent and appeals to charity are being made in earnest. Council officers are helping in this but apparently see little prospect for either rehousing or more money from the council.

At a time of economic recession and cutbacks, semi-alternatives like the Centre are particularly vulnerable. Had the wider economic situation not taken us over when it did, we might just have been able to establish ourselves more firmly and be sure of survival. As it is, survival is far from certain. Necessity this year has meant a reduction in the number of places available to parents who cannot work on the rota because of full-time employment, although it makes it possible for all parents who work on the rota to work part time.

In spite of its economic problems it seems that the Centre's general atmosphere is very good and relationships between people better than ever before, which presumably means there is more common interest. Parents stay and chat when they collect their children and they easily form friendships. The meetings are attended with interest if not always participation, but this always takes time. The polarity between the involved and the uninvolved of former years seems reduced, probably by having almost everyone working on the rota. Ideology is hardly discussed and so another area of dissent ceases to exist; this may mean that the discussions of earlier years were far too self-conscious and frightening in their implied judgments - although I am not prepared to admit that in principle discussion should be limited because it is frightening. The constant probings and attempts to analyse and record what has happened have been important both to those of us involved and also to forewarn other people who may attempt similar projects.

However, it is clear that the Centre provides more than ever for a drastic need in parents as well as in children, and the support people/women gain from being able to share their problems instead of being isolated at home with their children is crucial. But how will the present group cope with the threat of closure? Will their unity and common need enable them to find some solution? One sincerely hopes so. By June almost all the old people will have left. There will be yet more staff changes. When a full-time worker's job was advertised recently it brought over sixty applicants, which reflects the level of unemployment as much as it reflects the desirability of working at the Centre.

I have to think very carefully about what to say in conclusion. My first thought was to stress very emphatically to anyone now thinking of starting a community nursery how important it is for their own survival to be properly and permanently financed. I want to say: 'Do not accept an annually renewable grant; do not accept voluntary labour unless it is in addition to a full paid staff. We know that a system of voluntary labour can discriminate against women who work full time. We know that it undermines the struggles of nursery workers, and most of all we know the cost of doing the council's work for them.' But what if refusing to accept these conditions means you don't get anything?. We also know the stress that most women with young children are under and how much the Children's Community Centre has helped and changed so many people. So I cannot say emphatically - don't do it - I can say only that if you have no alternative, at least be aware of its implications and consider other needs as well as your own.

I believe we should insist on having control and involvement (if we want it) in any nursery in order to make sure it satisfies our needs and practises the sort of child care we want. But first we need nurseries, and these are still a long way off.

Work done in community groups such as the Centre means we have a much clearer idea of what we want. The women's movement has provided vital material on the subject. We can no longer look at nurseries purely from the 'education of the child' point of view. We now know a great deal about the needs of women and children. We know what changes we want in the working conditions of nursery workers and we know that men must take up their responsibility in the care and education of their own and all children. We talk of the millions of working mothers for whom lack of nurseries is a problem; but the millions of working fathers also have to see this as their problem, which it most certainly is. But the missing component as yet is the organised power to force the government and local councils to provide what we want and need. Many of these millions of working fathers are in the trade union movement - when are they going to apply their organised power to this problem? To insist on this is clearly an area of struggle for women trade unionists as well as all of us.

   We desperately need a campaign for nurseries to link up all the
isolated groups which are too vulnerable, too unstable. Community
groups, women's groups, nursery workers and trade union branches
need to be in contact with one another so that we do not make
conflicting demands which undermine each other. But, most
important, because we each bring a crucial segment to an enlight-
ened child care demand.

References

Not so much a Day Nursery, 'Spare Rib', no. 17 (from 9 Newburgh
Street, London W1A 4XS).
'Children's Community Centre', pamphlet no. 2 (from Children's
Community Centre, 123 Dartmouth Park Road, London N19).
'The Patter of Tiny Contradictions', 'Red Rag' no. 5, 1973 (from
22 Murray Mews, London NW1).
Film '123' (available from Liberation Films, 83 Belsize Lane,
London NW3; Concorde Films, Nackton, Ipswich, Suffolk; Contemporary
Films, 55 Greek Street, London W1).

5 A case study of child-minders in the London Borough of Camden

Elizabeth Urben

Women's main role has always been held to be the care of the home
and children. If they did work, it was mainly in menial jobs,
although a minority have always had good positions. It was only in
exceptional circumstances, such as wartime, that official recognition and support was given to them as workers. During World War
II, for example, women were seen to be of such value as workers
that many state nurseries were organised to allow more women to go
out to work. Since then, however, the number of nurseries has
rapidly declined but there has been no comparable decrease in the
number of working women with children.

Most women seek employment for financial reasons or to escape
the boredom and isolation of being shut in a flat or house with
little or no contact with anyone other than children during the day.
This latter situation has been aggravated by the breakdown of
established communities which has grown out of the greater mobility
of much of the population. In this society, the mother of a pre-
school child who goes out to work has to make arrangements for the
care of that child. The break-up of the extended family means
that alternative solutions have to be reached. Three options are
available - nursery schools, day nurseries and child-minders. Most
attention is focused on the provision of places at nursery schools
and day nurseries since the majority of these are council-run and
the teachers and nursery nurses are likely to have formal qualifications. Nursery schools are the responsibility of Education
Authorities and usually take children from the age of three upwards.
Day nurseries accept children from about six months old and are
under the Social Services Department. Both, therefore, are firmly
structured into the provisions local authorities make available for
working mothers.

The child-minder is a woman who looks after someone else's child
during the day for payment, accepting conditions that many of the
women are trying to escape from by working. Such women have a long
history of service, but they first came to the notice of law-makers
in the mid-nineteenth century. It was not until 1948, however, that
any legal controls over child-minders were established and they were
required to be registered by the local health authority. A main
contributory factor for this was World War II and the increase in the

number of mothers who worked and whose children were placed in situations where they were not protected by existing legislation. Since 1971, the Social Services Departments have been responsible for the registration of child-minders, but this has been seen more as a form of control than of support.

The attraction of the child-minder for the local authority is that there is no need for special premises or special equipment. Nor is it necessary to make arrangements for providing food or employing specially trained staff. Child-minding also avoids the necessity of assessing the fees to be paid by the mother on the basis of her means. This is particularly relevant in the present economic situation when day nurseries and nursery schools are no longer expanding their places. The child-minder can too easily be seen as a cheap alternative to nurseries for young children and, in many ways, as a second-rate alternative to a nursery nurse, lacking her training and having even less financial reward. It is important to consider whether child-minders should be viewed by the public like this. Do they not provide a form of more individual care which is particularly suitable for babies and younger children, as well as some children until they attend school? Child-minders therefore, have a greater service to offer than is often acknow-ledged and more consideration should be given to the possibility of setting up a two-tier system which includes both child-minders and nursery places. Support for nursery schools and day nurseries should not mean the exclusion of child-minders from similar action, but their association in joint campaigns. It is crucial at the same time to establish proper links between the two spheres - to enable child-minders to train as nursery nurses, etc., so that child-minders are not reinforced in their role as the cheap solu-tion - the second best and most exploited solution to the problems of day care for the under-fives.

As has been shown, local authorities have minimal control over child-minders and their conditions of work compared with their responsibility for day nurseries. Despite this, there are many more unregistered child-minders than registered and in the past few years the public image of the child-minder has always been that of the unregistered minder. In 1975, increased national publicity was given to the danger of leaving children with minders. This occurred at a time when more women were beginning to work in order to help support their families financially. This movement affected the child-minding situation in two ways. On the one hand, there was an increased demand for child-minding facilities. On the other hand, more women were likely to consider child-minding as a way of supplementing the family income and so become home workers, with all the disadvantages and problems of isolation, exploitation and lack of protection that this entails.

In some instances, however, there are movements to overcome this. One London borough was reported to be setting up a pilot scheme for employing child-minders. In another London borough, a Child-minders' Action Group had become members of the National Union of Public Employees. NUPE has produced a briefing paper on child-minders and approved a 'Childminders' Charter', which among other items calls for:

(a) Direct employment of childminders by the local authority

(b)   A substantial increase in the rates of pay and improvements
      in conditions of service
(c)   Training for all childminders in aspects of child care
(d)   Greatly improved communications between local authorities
      and the childminder
(e)   Proper guidance to be given to both parents and childminders
      on their responsibilities.

On the other hand, the Union is also aware of several obstacles to
recruiting substantial numbers of minders. The major one is the
isolation of child-minders, particularly from their colleagues. In
other words, this study was concerned to explore the problems of
child-minders as a potential group of women in the community in their
own right, rather than from the usual perspective of the working
mothers who depend upon their services.

These different aspects of child-minding - their bad image, their
isolation, the experimental schemes of support - were borne in mind
when embarking on the survey of some of the child-minders in Camden.
Most studies of child-minders have been looking at them from the
consumer's point of view, that is from the parents' position, with
comments and criticisms being made of the services provided by the
child-minder. It was decided, therefore, that this study should be
aimed at the child-minders: their thoughts on their position and
the conditions in which they work. Camden was chosen because it is
one of the London boroughs that has been very conscious of its
responsibilities to its child-minders. The time factor combined
with the high degree of co-operation from the Social Services
Department meant that the survey concentrated on registered minders
only. This affected their circumstances, especially their relationship with the Social Services Department. A brief résumé of the
major findings of the survey will help to highlight the conditions
under which child-minders work. In some respects, however, these
are no different from those of any woman who has to look after a
child under five: that of coping with housework, a family and
caring for the child throughout the day. In these ways, then, the
child-minder represents an extreme case of women's exploitation in
our society - isolated in a subordinate and economically dependent
role tied to her image as the housewife and mother. Over them all
is the ideal of the super-efficient housewife and mother, and yet
ironically, by the same mythology, she is also associated with the
reverse - the classic image of the child-minder.

For the classic image of the child-minder is very different from
that of a mother. She is seen as a woman who looks after about a
dozen children, giving them as little as possible in order to bring
in as much money as possible. Yet this was certainly not the situation among these minders. Half of them minded only one child.
Three minders looked after more than three children under five years
old, including their own, but even then the most children recorded
for one minder was five. These low numbers, so different from the
public picture, were due mainly to the fact that a registered minder
in Camden may take in no more than three children under five. Very
few of the group took up child-minding as a way of earning good
money. The major reasons given for starting were the ability to
work at home and earn from home, that they liked children, that
someone asked them, and the need for company for their own child.

This last reason was often given by the minder who had her youngest child left at home when the others had gone to school. It was clear that a number of minders had discovered only by accident, for example a Health Visitor told them, that they should be registered with the local authority if they were paid to look after someone else's child.

The two most important conditions for any worker are hours and pay. Child-minders are no exception to this. Minders could expect children to come to their home from 7.30 a.m. onwards and to leave any time up to 7 p.m. As a result, most child-minders worked forty hours or more a week. The question of how long a child stayed with the minder was one of the areas that caused most anxiety between parents and minders, since many minders felt that parents exploited them by leaving the child longer than was necessary. One minder, for example, was left with a child until 11 p.m. without any explanation from the parents. It was very obvious in this instance that the minder was most concerned at how the child felt, having been left with the minder beyond her usual hour for going home. As many of the women started minding to provide company for her own child rather than for the money, a late departure of a minded child meant disruption both to the child and the minder's family, nor did it mean any increase in money on the grounds of overtime.

The other area of concern, that of payment, is one of great complexity. Among these minders there was a great disparity in the rates charged, from £2.50 to £6 per week, full time and usually inclusive of food, but with no consensus on the question of paying for a child's absence or over holiday periods. Some minders were able to ask for money in advance, a recommendation made by the Social Services Department, and a retainer fee, but others found this difficult without any apparent official support. Most of the minders earned between £3 and £10 per week. Two earned over £15, but both of these minders cared for more than three children. The low incomes recorded, compared with those attributed to the illegal child-minders, reflect the contact with the Social Services Department which restricts the number of children to be cared for. What these amounts mean in terms of increased money for the family budget is described by one minder. She had worked out that, taking into account electricity, heating and food, the profit from charging £4 per week for one child was 5 new pence. In spite of the difficulties of payment and the inadequacy, in most cases, of gaining a reasonable income from child-minding, less than a quarter of the minders interviewed welcomed the idea of employment by the local authority. The majority were unwilling to exchange their freedom for what they saw as the bondage of tax and National Insurance. This is understandable since very few of the women saw minding as a job, in the same way as they saw factory work, for instance. But looking at child-minding as an occupation, since it is a paid occupation, it means that minders are in a very poor economic position and without the security and protection that most women workers have. At a time when employment policies are changing, through the introduction of equal pay and the Sex Discrimination Act, child-minders, like other women, need to be encouraged to look at the long-term consequences of their position. This may well lead

to direct employment by local authorities, as advocated by NUPE, and
to a clearer relationship between child-minding and nursery
facilities.

As part of the aim of looking at the job from the child-minder's
point of view, she was asked about the advantages and disadvantages
of her work. Very few minders had very definite views. When asked
what they liked about their job, the largest number said that they
liked children, and about equal numbers appreciated the extra money
and liked being their own boss. The main criticism of the job was
the unreliable hours. Three minders disliked the fact that the money
was also unreliable and a similar number was very definite about the
isolation that they experienced. Another disadvantage of the job is
the additional responsibility involved in looking after someone
else's child. Suggestions for making child-minding easier were
mainly practical, such as asking for help with paper and crayons or
the use of double baby buggies in order to get out more easily. A
few minders were concerned with less material aspects, for example
greater support from the Social Services Department and a leaflet
that could be given to the parents written from the minder's angle.
This was mentioned particularly because the Department provided a
leaflet describing what the parent can expect from the minder.
Here again the existing contact with the Social Services Department
affected their responses. Camden runs a toy library for child-
minders and lends out a limited number of baby buggies. As well as
helping, practically, the Department has also been providing more
intangible support and information. So these minders are more likely
to look to the Social Services Department for help in the problems
they face as child-minders than the majority of minders who have
little or no contact with a department.

One area that was looked at was the background of the children.
It is usually held that child-minders are of service to West Indian
and African mothers in particular, who are more used to an extended
family where children can be left with relations. Again, the image
of the mother who leaves her child with a child-minder is that of
the less-advantaged, single mother. In this case, however, the
majority of the children in the study were of British nationality
and only five were from one-parent families. Most of them were
either only children or had one sibling. Nearly all the minders
knew whether the mother worked - most did - and what sort of work she
did. The jobs mentioned ranged from lecturer, doctor and adoptions
officer to machinists, hospital workers and cleaners. Again this
shows that minders provide a positive service which some mothers
use from choice.

Finally, the minder's awareness and appreciation of group solidarity were explored. There was a fairly strong demand for some
form of contact between child-minders. In the interview they were
asked which they would prefer, an association or a union. The
expressed wish was for an association. The idea of joining a union,
such as NUPE, had no support as yet. Some minders felt that a union
would be too highly organised and others felt that they caused
nothing but trouble. For a group that is groping towards solidarity
it is understandable that a union still appears unattractive. It is
worth-while noting, however, that other minders have joined NUPE and
its membership among minders continues to increase.

It has been remarked upon that the Social Services Department
in Camden has shown a very positive approach to the child-minders
in its borough and this has been expressed in two schemes. On the
one hand, there are facilities for borrowing toys and equipment.
On the other hand, an 'in-service' training programme has been set
up to cover topics of interest to child-minders. This has been held
in the different areas in the borough and for many child-minders it
has meant an opportunity to meet their colleagues for the first
time. Once the training programme has been completed, monthly
meetings have been held and out of these has grown the Camden
Association of Childminders.

The Association, founded in October 1975, has nine elected
officers and a constitution. Its main object is 'to protect and
promote the interests and good image of the childminders in Camden'.
This aim has arisen out of the Association's awareness of the
criticism being levelled nationally at child-minders. Another
objective of the Association is to work closely with other agencies,
particularly the Social Services Department, involved in the welfare
of children in Camden. This already reflects a growing feeling of
their own worth, as the minders are able to offer their services
on an equal footing with these other agencies. The Association is
also concerned to provide support, both educational and social,
for its own members. The Association is already showing signs of
its effectiveness, since a representative from the Social Services
says: 'We are already getting more people who want to be minders
through the publicity of the Association.'

Although still in its early days, the Association is looking at
areas which cause most concern to minders. It is planning a
Minder's Charter outlining the minder's expectations for the parents
of minded children. It will not, however, include any recommendations on rates of pay. Another area which the Association is
exploring is that of insurance cover. At the present time,
minders are very vulnerable should there be any damage or accident
as a result of their job. The Association has not yet established
a regular pattern of meetings but, aware of the difficulties minders
have in travelling any distance with several children, they plan to
overcome this by meeting on a rota basis in the different areas.

Apart from these practical issues, the organisation could be of
value to the child-minders because they themselves are working out
what areas and concerns are important to them. The opportunity to
meet together should help to reduce the child-minder's feeling of
isolation and weakness in making demands. Even where a minder cannot
meet others regularly, she will have a charter that states what she
can expect of a child's parents and a group with officials to whom
she can turn for support and advice. The establishment of the
Association is an important step in the recognition of child-minders
as a valuable resource in the care of the pre-school child in
Camden. It is also of particular value in that the child-minders
are organising for themselves. Although still linked to the Social
Services Department for advice and support, these minders are now
becoming more assertive and independent. This is a significant step
in terms of the national attitude to them, since they are showing
themselves to be a responsible group of people who should not be
downtrodden but have their own needs acknowledged and met. It is

important that this movement in Camden should appear as an inspira-
tion for other Social Services Departments and child-minders to
explore ways of developing their own local support groups and,
ultimately, allowing them to produce a more national movement.

6 The housing struggles of two women

Jan O'Malley

The struggles described here involve two North Kensington women, Maggie O'Shannon and Merle Major. Maggie is Irish and has two children, Merle is West Indian and has six. In both households the woman was the head of the household and men never played more than a secondary subordinate position and were never relied on. Both women lived on social security during these years of housing struggle.

However, they were not isolated in their struggle. Both made demands for strong supportive action from the local organisations they knew of in the area. Maggie involved both branches of the Notting Hill People's Association, the Lancaster Neighbourhood Centre and the People's Centre; she had developed the idea of squatting from the squats in luxury blocks organised by the People's Association squatters' group a few weeks before, in December 1968. Merle lived next door to the Notting Hill Community Workshop in St Ervans Road, W 10, whose members were closely involved with the People's Association and so ensured that the energy of all members was put into backing Merle's struggle.

THE STRUGGLE OF MAGGIE O'SHANNON

Maggie lived in Camelford Road, a street in the Lancaster Road West redevelopment area of North Kensington. It was at a public meeting on the redevelopment scheme in July 1967 that several of the voci-ferous Irish women from Camelford Road, including Maggie, first made their anger felt. Members of the Lancaster Neighbourhood Centre went down and talked with them the next day. Their anger was focused on the remoteness of the plans from the needs of people like themselves. For example, there was to be one nursery in the scheme for fifty children. There were over that number of children in their street alone.

It was not till the spring of 1968 that half a dozen members of the Centre went down to Camelford Road again with the aim that a campaign should be waged to involve the whole street in a protest against the dreadful conditions its tenants were forced to endure. The first street meeting was held in mid-July 1968, and at this a

street committee of five was elected and the priorities of the
street were decided: rehousing for all those in the worst conditions, before the official date of 1973. It was decided to hold
another street meeting, but this time with tables and typewriters
in the street, so that a start could be made in drawing up the list
of all those in need of priority rehousing, and of all the repairs
which had to be done. The street committee had agreed that a
formal letter of complaint should be sent for each tenant to the
Town Hall, listing the repairs outstanding and the urgency of
rehousing. In October these letters were finally handed in to the
Town Hall, fully documenting the urgent repairs needed in Camelford
Road. This was backed up by a centre-page spread of the local
newspaper featuring Camelford Road that week. Council investiga-
tions followed and some repairs were carried out as a result of
Council pressure on landlords.

Whereas most of the action in 1968 was focused on the issue of
repairs, in 1969 the emphasis shifted to rehousing. Early in
January 1969 the Council held a public meeting to explain the
redevelopment scheme to the people of the area. In advance of the
meeting the news had been leaked through 'People's News' that the
rehousing of people in Camelford Road had been put off until 1975
as a result of the street having been shifted from phase 3 to phase
5 of the redevelopment scheme. Spurred by this news as well as by
her own appalling housing conditions, one of the tenants of Camelford Road, Maggie O'Shannon, decided to squat with her family in
no. 7 Camelford Road - the best house in the street and empty for
nearly a year.

Maggie described the factors which led to her decision to squat -
first her housing conditions:

> The lavatory from the flat above flushed straight into the
> kitchen. There was sometimes 3 inches of sewage in the place.
> The house produced £20 a week rent, but there were no repairs
> done. The agent said he couldn't do any without a letter from
> the landlord, and he lived in the south of France. Why should he
> bother? If we didn't pay the rent, the next tenant would ...

Maggie was right. Soon after she moved out to squat she discovered
that her old basement had been let to a West Indian woman and four
children, at amost double the rent, and still no repairs done. She
went on to explain how, over the months at the beginning of 1968,
people from the Centre started coming into the street and talking
with the tenants.

> I began to ask myself, why should I live like this? The Council
> was no help at all. The Chairman of the Housing Committee is a
> woman who is a real working-class Tory. She has our
> lives in her hands. We're pleading with her to help us, to give
> our children somewhere to live. In August 1968 I noticed that
> the house across the way was empty and had been a long time. I
> said to myself, I'll squat in it.

> The real decider came when I asked this woman when I
> could move out of my basement and she said it would not be for at
> least another five years. I then approached the People's
> Association and asked them if they would help me move into no. 7.

> For three weeks we prepared - we had to get stocks of coal
> and food in, arrange for electricity from another house, water,

guards and the rest of it. Everyone in the neighbourhood
knew, but nobody told. I moved in at 8 a.m. one morning in
January and by 8.05 all my things were across and the house
barricaded.

Maggie did not know who owned the house when she moved in, but by
a piece of political luck it turned out to belong to the Greater
London Council, the very authority which had the responsibility for
rehousing the street. She had picked a perfect pawn in the bargaining game. From the start, Maggie made it clear that she was not
squatting just to get herself rehoused sooner. 'We said we'd be
the last in the street to be rehoused. We also said they [the
authorities] should bring the rehousing date forward from 1975
which it was, to this year [i.e. 1969],' she declared. Within a
week she was joined by another woman, Bridie Matthews, and her
family, and together they put out a Squatters' Charter on 24
January to make their position clear:

We see our act as the first step in a fight for better conditions
for all the people of Camelford Road and the Lancaster Road
(West) Redevelopment area. If we are allowed to remain in no. 7,
we are prepared to be the last families to be rehoused from
Camelford Road.

The Charter went on to demand permanent tenancies for both their
families and the immediate delivery of full information on the
phasing of the redevelopment and the time of rehousing to every
tenant in the area, including a guarantee that everyone who so
wished would be rehoused in North Kensington. The Charter was
presented to the Greater London Council, the Inner London Education
Authority and the Royal Borough of Kensington and Chelsea.

Huge white letters were painted on the street outside the house –
'This is Maggie's and Bridie's house. Defend it.' Frequent street
meetings were held with Maggie addressing the crowd on the street
through a loud hailer from the top window of her new home. She
ended one of her speeches with the following words: 'When they do
come to evict us, they'll have as big a fight as we do to get a
Council house – and you know how hard that is.'

Many of the tenants from Camelford Road joined with Maggie and
Bridie in a visit to the Kensington Council meeting at the end of
January. They felt it was important that the Council should be made
to feel what it was like to live in Camelford Road. They collected
choice pickings from the rot of Camelford Road: a jar of rain water
which had fallen in 15 minutes through the ceiling of a bedroom;
a large piece of paper from a kitchen ceiling sodden with overflow
from the toilet above; wallpaper which had fallen off a bedroom wall
because of damp. All these, well labelled, were banged down onto the
highly polished tables where the Councillors sat. This alone,
together with Maggie's speech, was enough for the order to clear the
Chamber to be given, and the Mayor, mace and Councillors began to
beat a hasty retreat. On the way out, the largest parcel of all, a
stinking parcel of old rubbish which had been left by the Council
outside a basement flat where five children had recently moved in,
was presented to the porter, labelled 'For the Mayor' and the group
left the Town Hall, shouting, 'We'll be back!' As she was being
hustled out, Maggie retorted: 'What do you mean, leave? These are
the people you should ask to leave,' she continued, pointing to the

crowd of Councillors who were rapidly withdrawing from the
Chamber; all because one of the citizens of the Royal Borough had
raised her voice in a Council meeting and had actually presented
material evidence of the rotting conditions of parts of the
Royal Borough.

Early in February the first official response was made by the
Chairman of the GLC Housing Committee:

The property is owned by the GLC but held by the ILEA. It has
been represented as unfit for human habitation by the Royal
Borough and is included in a confirmed CPO [Compulsory Purchase
Order] made by the Borough. It is expected that the site will
be required by the ILEA for the rebuilding of a primary
school ... in the meantime the premises must be cleared as
soon as possible ...

However, on 5 March Maggie had a GLC rent book shoved through
the letterbox, for the rent of the whole house, together with a
statement from the GLC that they could stay in no. 7 which, though
technically unfit, was better than their previous homes. Maggie's
response to this was firm:

The struggle was for Camelford Road. This statement just sorts
out the squatters and makes no mention of the road. Neither
Mrs. Matthews nor me would be happy with getting a tenancy here
and forgetting the rest of the street.

A few days after getting the rent book, Maggie and Bridie were out
organising another street meeting in Camelford Road about how to
mount pressure for the whole of the street to be rehoused within the
year by the GLC. It was agreed, as a first step, to draw up a petition signed by every tenant in the street.

However, by 23 March, the fight had been won. The GLC announced
that rehousing would begin in Camelford Road and the adjacent
streets in a few months, but would probably take a year to complete.
No distinction was to be made between the rehousing of furnished and
unfurnished tenants.

On 1 June the first three families moved out, and by the end of
1970 only one family was left. The O'Sullivans, a family with
twelve children, seemed to have been forgotten. Maggie and Bridie
rushed back to the area and gave a seven-day ultimatum to the
authorities. If the family was not rehoused by then, they would be
forced to consider direct action again. The O'Sullivans were
rehoused within the week.

So effective action was taken by the people of Camelford Road,
under the leadership of Maggie O'Shannon, to force the authorities
to take account of the housing needs of the local people and to speed
up their rehousing and that of the people in the neighbouring streets
by five years. However, in achieving this, the people inevitably
destroyed their own organising network and were scattered to Council
housing estates throughout London. Small groups of tenants did
manage to get rehoused together, but a friendship rather than an
organising network was sustained.

THE STRUGGLE OF MERLE MAJOR

In May 1971 Merle Major decided she had lived at 62 St Ervans Road for long enough. She was fed up with private landlords and was going to squat in a Council flat to make the Council face her housing problem once and for all.

Since March 1968, when she moved into no. 62, she had experienced almost every Council department and their fumbling inaction. Her problem was quite clear. She had taken the two rooms at the top of this house because she was desperate after being evicted by another landlord. She had five children at the time, the back room leaked so much that they all had to sleep in the front room despite the gaping hole in the wall by the window. The Children's Department response had been to take all her children into care eight years before, because of the bad housing conditions in which they were living. However, they never did anything about the bad housing. They did not even make sure Merle was on the housing list. The Public Health Department had been visiting the house since 1964 when the landlord had bought it, but never succeeded in forcing the necessary repairs. The family in the basement was left without a roof on the kitchen for eighteen months. The whole house had dangerous wiring which caused fires on more than one occasion.

Before Merle moved in, the other tenants had started to fight back. In October 1967 the basement tenants, the Wrights, won an important test case to get themselves reclassified from furnished to unfurnished tenants, so gaining greater security. They then got their rent cut by the Rent Officer from £4.50 to £1.50. Another tenant on the first floor, Ann Worsfold, had followed their lead. She became an unfurnished tenant and got her rent cut from £6 to £2.37½. Merle had taken her two rooms at the ridiculous figure of £8.50. The Rent Tribunal cut this to £7.50, but as long as she was a furnished tenant she had no security. In May 1969 the landlord gave her notice to quit, which she successfully fought by getting reclassified as unfurnished. The Court also awarded her damages for the bad living conditions, and imposed a 28-day repair order on the landlord. Her rent was then cut by the Rent Officer to £2.37½. The landlord appealed, only to have it cut further to £2. So, together, the tenants had made a big hole in the landlord's receipts, cutting them from the original total of £19 for the three floors to £6.25 a week. He did not take this assault on his income lightly. In 1967 he had tried his hand at illegal eviction, throwing all Ann Worsfold's possessions on the street while she was out. The Council was pressed to prosecute, although this resulted in a fine of only £25 for the landlord, which obviously did not deter him.

In May 1970 he was at it again. Merle and Ann had gone shopping together one Tuesday afternoon. Ten minutes later they came back to find the front door boarded up, a furniture van waiting and keys nailed to the door with a note telling them that they had moved to Wandsworth to a house they had never heard of! An angry crowd gathered, together with horse, cart and battering-ram to force in the boarded-up door. But negotiations started instead, and four hours of police/solicitor bargaining with the landlord eventually resulted in the tenants going back in, only to find furniture thrown downstairs, clothing stuffed into boxes and many doors off their hinges.

But the street was angry. Eighty-five residents of St Ervans Road immediately signed a petition demanding that the Council take no. 62 off the landlord's hands. The People's Centre and the Golborne Social Rights Committee organised a march in June to the Town Hall, led by Merle and Ann, demanding (among other things) that the Council should take over no. 62. The Council response? They accepted that the management was bad and the conditions filthy but could do nothing because of the uncertain future of the area.

But the landlord had not finished. Later in June he took off the front door and locked it in the basement, leaving the tenants to break into the basement and rehang the door. Then, after a few months had elapsed, in February 1971, he and his brother attacked Merle one Sunday morning, and brought up stinking rubbish from the basement and threw it all over her kitchen. The night before, he had cut the electricity off. In March the ground-floor tenant found a microphone under the bed connected to the basement, and the landlord sitting on a chair in the middle of her room in the dark. A week later she was locked out. On both these occasions the Law Centre acted with great speed to obtain injunctions against the landlord: one to stop him going into Merle's flat or interfering with her in any way, the other to make him allow Maureen, the ground floor tenant, back in her flat. These injunctions were served on the landlord within 24 hours of the Court granting them, by a People's Association member - in contrast to the Council who had taken nine months to serve a summons on him for his illegal eviction in May of 1970. In April 1971 he was fined £200 and £60 costs for harassing, assaulting and illegally evicting Merle, thanks to the Law Centre and People's Association energy in speeding up the legal machinery.

This was the background against which Merle decided to squat. She had tried all the legal remedies open to her. However heavily the landlord was fined, however much she got the rent cut, however often she called in the Health Inspectors, she still did not have enough room to have all her children back home; the repairs were still not done, and she still had to live with an ever-present landlord. There was just no knowing what he would do next.

So she asked the People's Association Housing Group to find her an empty Council flat in which she would squat. No. 11 Powis Square, a newly converted Council basement, was found and in May Merle moved in with the three of her children she had managed to recover from the Children's Department, and another child nearly a year old. Merle informed the Council of her demands: a decent home for herself and all her family; the compulsory purchase of 62 St Ervans Road.

Once in, Merle proceeded to organise a People's Rally the coming Sunday afternoon. She involved a steel band, and people with guitars, mouth-organs and tambourines. She wrote songs and built an effigy of her landlord for the occasion. Starting out from 62 St Ervans Road, which she described in detail as 'the house of horrors', she led a swaying and dancing procession around the streets chanting rhythmically, 'Get involved, get involved, Power to the People, get involved.' Once in Powis Square, the steel band struck up, and Merle then climbed up on a ledge and told the 500 people there her story. After a massive show of hands in support of the squat, and pledges to come and support her if eviction attempts were made, Merle

stepped down and set fire to her effigy of the landlord. Then
there was more music and Merle sang the song she had written:

MERLE'S SONG, 'FIRE IN THE HOLE'

There's fire, fire in the hole.
Let the people explode with human emotion.
You know there is fire, fire in the hole.
Let the people explode all over this land.
You may be able to kill somebody dead,
You may be able to bust their head,
But you can't kill emotion;
You can't kill human emotion.

Man, woman, man take the people's hand,
Open up your big food bin,
Let the people in.
To have your corpse all running like that
While the people are homeless
It's a sin.
Let my brothers and sisters come on in.
You fool - going to blow over,
Going to bust your building down;
Going to tear your building down to the ground.

The people are the wheels that run your car,
The people of the Borough pay for your car,
The people do everythin', everythin',
The people brought you your strength;
They fight your war.
The poor men ain't fighting no wars no more
Unless it's for their own salvation
To help their own dedication.

Remember when you were fighting for your independence
You said that you were right, right day and night,
Dying don't mean nothing, dying is living,
And living is dying just across the river,
And nobody's scared of dying no more.
It's better to be dead than to live on and be scared.
It's better to be dead than to live on and be scared.
Fire, fire in the hole.

Within two weeks of her squatting the Council responded to Merle's
demands. The Housing Chairman called for special reports from his
officers on 62 St Ervans Road and said the Council were prepared to
go all the way to using a CPO if it was needed. Council negotiations brought an offer of a six-roomed house for Merle from the
Kensington Housing Trust; initially for a period of six months,
since the house was due for demolition. At the end of eight weeks
of squatting Merle decided to accept the offer, to get all her
children back and recover her strength for another fight in six
months' time if necessary. But the demolition was delayed and Merle
got a transfer at the end of a year to a newer Trust property.

In July the Council announced their decision to put a CPO on 62 St Ervans Road - the first time ever that the Council had used their powers against a landlord because of his harassment and bad management. But their heart wasn't in it, and they produced a very insubstantial case to the Ministry for the CPO. Meanwhile the land-lord got to work with a paint-brush, put in a few sticks of furni-ture, and re-let the floors at £13 a week. He got single short-stay tenants from West End agencies who left rather than put up a fight. In October 1971 the new tenants moved in, but within only a few weeks they were reduced to sleepless wrecks by the landlord and his brother's constant presence in the house, moving stealthily about till 3 or 4 a.m., banging, knocking, footsteps stopping out-side the door. The girls downstairs took to sleeping with friends, and came back with mattresses to find their water-heater smashed with a meat-hook hanging beside it and a crucifix with a skull and crossbones on it outside their door. They confronted the landlord's brother, who admitted he'd been through the room but that it was common practice. Five of the six tenants were too scared to do anything but move out, making way for the next wave of tenants.

All this was going on after the CPO had been put on the house, and while the Minister was considering it. When the Inspector came to visit, the landlord showed him round, and all the tenants were out. Ignoring the long history of harassment and bad conditions, the Inspector was taken in by the touch of the landlord's paint-brush. He turned down the CPO, saying that the internal and exter-nal conditions of the ground and first floors were satisfactory and that there were plans for the whole area to be compulsorily purchased shortly by the GLC and there were therefore no grounds for taking no. 62 out of turn! True enough, the GLC did put a CPO on the area in 1973, but this still left the landlord with far more years of grace than he deserved.

But despite the delaying action of the Ministry, Merle's deci-sion to squat forced the Council to take two actions which years of legal actions, Health Inspectors and social workers' visits had not achieved: to put a CPO on no. 62 and to find Merle a six-roomed house to live in. This was an experience of power and political effectiveness which was entirely new to Merle, who had for years been on the receiving end in relation to the authorities, whether receiv-ing Social Security or having her children taken into care. It had a lasting effect in terms of the way she saw herself in relation to the authorities. She had a new confidence and assertiveness of her needs and demands and a real awareness that the authorities - be they Social Security, the Housing Trust or the Council - are there to be your servants and not to dictate your needs.

As well as providing an important political experience for Merle as the squatter, the whole event provided a focus for the work of the People's Association Housing Group in the Colville area for the two months the squat lasted. It meant that all day, every day, members of the Housing Group combined guard duty at the squat with continuous discussion on the street about the issues raised by the squat - ownership of property, compulsory purchase, and what had to be done if speculators were to be stopped in the area.

In terms of the housing battle-ground, the demand for the com-pulsory purchase of no. 62 related to a property outside the Colville

area where the battle between speculators and non-profit ownership
was most intense, but to force the Council to use a CPO on this one
house increased the possibility of them being forced to use their
powers of compulsory purchase in the Colville area too.

In both of these struggles, Merle and Maggie showed how women who
are not employed at the point of production can and do involve themselves in political struggle focused on the issue of getting decent
housing. For them both, their housing had the special importance
that their home was both their workplace and their home. Both
women resisted the danger of fighting a purely individualistic
struggle and made a determined effort to make it a collective
struggle of all those in the area who were involved in the fight for
a decent home. In challenging the authority of the private landlord and the Council over the quality of housing provided, they
both gained direct political experience of how to deal with bureaucratic indifference, professional incompetence and open bullying,
and learned the importance of collective organisation in the
struggle to assert their needs over the official criteria of housing
need and private profit.

Note

This article is to be included in Jan O'Malley, 'Community Struggles
in North Kensington', Spokesman Books, Nottingham, 1977.

7 **When women get involved in community action**

Cynthia Cockburn

This chapter is based upon conversations that took place between myself and three other women in 1975. They were for use in a local community newspaper. (1) All three were housewives with children, living in poorly maintained council housing in south London. All had been activists around housing conditions in their neighbourhood or on their estate. (I too am a mother and have been an activist - but I also do paid work.) We were exploring what happens to a woman's family life and relationships when she becomes involved outside the home. What are the gains and what are the losses for her? And the questions that are the other side of the coin: what barriers does a woman's domestic life put up against her involvement outside, and do they determine the sort of action she can take?

At the time of the Housing Finance Act of 1972 many 'street groups' and tenants' associations were formed or re-activated to fight against the proposed 'fair rents' system and the rent increases that would ensue. Jan Kirk helped to form a tenants' association on the run-down council estate where she and her family live. She and others leafleted the tenants to call meetings to discuss the implications of the Act for their estate. They decided to clog the appeals machinery by encouraging all tenants to refuse to accept assessments and later to withold proposed increases in a concerted rent strike. The tenants' association also took action over empty flats; on one occasion squatting a homeless family on the estate.

Joan Meader became involved in protests over conditions in the street where she lives, when a Neighbourhood Council was set up in the area and was able to offer support to such activities. The council and British Rail (which owned one side of the street) had allowed the place to become a tip for rubbish. Dorothy Harrison also first became involved in action through a street group of this kind that formed around housing problems. Later, when she moved into a council flat on an old and depressing estate, she formed a group of ten women to press for transfers and to protest over delayed repairs.

The conversations with Jan, Joan and Dorothy made me think anew about the purpose of women's unpaid domestic work, and the way it affects our experience: because that experience, the sort of way of life we are forced into as wives and mothers, has a direct effect on

our political ways of acting, whether this is in community action
or in industrial action around our paid jobs. So I want to put
forward some of these ideas as a context for the conversations
that follow.

All but a few women are domestic workers. Whatever other work
we do, either for enjoyment or for a wage, most of us are also
unpaid workers in the home. The first experience of liberating
change for many women, and the first step of revolutionary change
for women as a whole, is making contact with others outside the
home, on the basis of some shared problem. The first action women
take together may be leafleting round the estate to co-operate on a
complaint to the council about repairs. It may be getting mothers
and children together to sit down on the main road to demand a
pedestrian crossing. It may be, like Joan in the conversations that
follow, taking direct action against rats: 'You put the rat in the
jar, I'll screw the lid on and we'll both take it up to the town
hall.' Women often play a primary part in community action because
it is about things they know they know best about. As Joan says,
in a housing situation that is a health hazard, the woman is more
likely to act than the man because she lives there all day and
because she is impelled by fear for her children. Community action
of this kind is a significant phase of class struggle, but it is
also an element of women's liberation.

Women who have young children often work 24 hours a day. This
is no exaggeration. If a social worker or a doctor has to stay
'on call' all night, as a mother does, for instance, if she has
young children, that vigilance is called work, and is paid for.
Mothers put more labour power into domestic work than most other
women. But single women, childless wives and women in paid work
outside the home normally also put in several hours of work a day
in their own house or flat, cooking, cleaning, buying and repairing. Whether the woman is only repairing and maintaining herself
or is also servicing a man, or caring for the old, or the sick or
her children, she is doing work for the system as a whole. So
women are the people who, in the main, do the maintenance job for
capitalism - getting the worker back on the job, getting the child
disciplined and trained, caring for the casualties.

Women's domestic work has long been thought of as a 'use value',
something found, free as air. Now we understand that her labour
gives it potential exchange value. She could, in theory, ask for
payment for her labour in the home because she is helping to create
wealth. (2) She seems to work for her husband and for her children.
But if we see her husband as an employee of a firm, and her
children as trainee workers, we see that her real boss is her husband's boss and children's future employers.

The wife and mother, though, does not get paid for the work she
does for these distant, but quite real, employers. She gets money
for the materials she uses: that is the housekeeping money that
her husband gives her. But this is just as though a joiner were
given an advance to buy timber and screws. He will also get paid
for the time he puts in, but with rare exceptions a woman's domestic labour power is not paid for. It is not part of what the boss
gives her husband, or he gives her.

The woman's main service to capitalism - the service for which she

does not get paid - is 'reproducing the forces of production'. (3)
In this she is assisted and supervised by local state agencies whose
main role, too, among all the other functions of the state, is a
reproductive one. The local authority runs the schools, the social
services, the housing services.

It may be impossible to understand the political action of women
unless we understand two things. She is in the front line of interaction with the local state. When someone has to go and see the
schoolteacher about the truant child, when someone has to answer
the door to the social worker, or go and face the music at the rent
office: it's the woman. (4)

Women are also, incidentally, in the front line of interaction
with capital in its distributive guise. They are the shoppers.
Apart from beer and fags, the household necessities in most families
are bought by women.

Two particular problems arise for a woman because of her domestic
experience, and these are her basic realities. One is that she is
more or less isolated. The other is that she also cares. The
housewife normally does things alone - cleans out the bath, mends
the clothes, makes her contribution to the capitalist economy,
within the four walls that enclose her workplace and no one else's.
This is what women's movement writers have meant by 'privatisation'.

Second, though, a woman is always doing whatever she does for
another reason, which she often takes to be the only reason:
because she loves the people whom she looks after. The leftist
leaflet may say that she services the workforce. As far as she is
concerned she looks after her husband, 'Nan' and the kids. So
women as domestic workers are caught in the pincers of a contradiction. We, the mothers and lovers who care, are at the exact
point where all the good values of love and relationship are twisted,
manipulated and threatened by the economic function of the family.

What effect does this domestic experience of women have on their
outward actions? We can be seen to act at two levels; the level
of unconscious reaction (alone), and consciously (together). At
both levels we can see in our actions a reflection of the experience out of which they are born. At the unconscious and isolated
level we take terrible personal risks - 'unreliability' in paid
work, nagging at home, even in shoplifting - because our caring gets
us into impossible positions with regard to the outside world.

When women do begin to act together, consciously, the kinds of
action they engage in still reflect the domestic experience that
lies behind them. Women's action is usually relatively spontaneous
and dramatic. After all, women's exploitation, whatever else it may
also be, is always physical. It should be expected that sometimes
too the response will be physical - from eighteenth-century bread
riots to twentieth-century terrorism.

Women in action tend to be intractable and uncompromising. An
82-year-old woman who had been active in struggles over pay and
conditions as a hospital worker told me: 'I think men are rather
conservative. They meet people half way. We'd agitate. They'd
put in a demand for us. Then they'd come back with a quarter of
what we'd asked for and think they'd done all right. Women have got
more go. We'll keep on rucking till we get what we want.' Women
are less conditioned than men to seek the small advances that the

employer or the state can easily afford to give.

Women also tend to be unexpected, to think up new ways of doing things. The impressive strike at Imperial Typewriters (in which Asian women took a big part) was against the combined forces of the Transport and General Workers' Union and the management, and it pioneered a new form of organising: the grievance meeting, a mass meeting of the entire strike force to speak out about what was wrong. (5) Women in the night cleaners' campaign in 1972 wanted more flexible ways of organising because of the impossible strait-jacket that their night-work, home-work and lack of sleep put them in. (And the union would not innovate with them.)

Women are often total in their demands. All people, women and men, experience many different kinds of oppression in their lives. They are producers and reproducers, workers and lovers. To protect himself from the pain of that, a man is able to split off the part of him that is exploited at work from the part of him that is exploited, by the same system, at home. In fact he will often turn round and do the exploiting at home on behalf of the system. But a woman who spends a lot of her time in the home, caring for others there, especially if she works outside the home too, cannot help but feel the all-round oppression and want to fight on many fronts at once. May Hobbs, a couple of years after the night cleaners' campaign in which she played a leading part, said to me: 'People always wanted me to speak about cleaners, nothing but that. That was a small part of it for me. I'm a woman. It's one big struggle, a woman's struggle, it's not just organising round our jobs but it's to do with housing, health, everything that affects you.'

Finally, whatever the action women get involved in, it always modifies, sometimes transforms, personal relationships at home - as the following conversation shows very clearly. When they feel that they are in a struggle they share with other women, and that it is not just for themselves, they are prepared to 'take on' their husbands or menfolk in a way they would not otherwise do. This changed or changing relationship and the emotional effects of it always show up in women's action. Even though in the long run they may gain from it, in the short run it costs women a lot to put husband and children second. The anxiety, doubt and willpower involved are carried by women into meetings; they add to the feel-ings expressed there, and account also for the spasmodic nature of women's struggle.

Dorothy Harrison was born in the West Indies. She is married and has two daughters, aged four and two, and lives in Brixton. She was a trainee nurse, but 'because it is more convenient for us all', she has given that up, and now works three hours a day in a local club for pre-school children. Joan Meader is married, has a four-year-old son, and lives in a private tenancy in south London. The issue that brought them both into collective action was their housing condi-tions. Joan and a friend organised a group to fight the authori-ties about the rat infestation of their street, but she became a better ratcatcher than they: she caught more than 100 in one year, and delivered a few of them alive to the council.

Cynthia: *Is there any special reason why women are getting involved in housing issues round here?*

J: It's got to be women, we're the only ones that can understand the problem. The men are out all day. Take the situation where I live. My husband would never have done anything about it. He didn't have to sit there with the rats running over his feet. They're out at work. Their minds are occupied with other things. If it's a health problem, you know it's your kids who are going to be ill if nothing's done.

Are women in any case better at organising together than men are?

J: On anything that involves the family - yes. You can get a group together. Men won't work together so well. They are too self-centred. In street groups, the ones I know of, it was all women.

If action on the estates and in the streets is going to grow - do you think it has to be women organising alone, without men?

D: No. Because men have more time. Of course they could give some of that time that they have to us. But they must be in these organisations too, with us, otherwise they won't understand our problems.

J: When we started the street group up, my husband as good as said, 'You won't get anything done, it's all women.'

D: But if you have a few intelligent women and can make a bit of time (it's time you need), you'll be successful. I don't think a man can do better than me. Not now.

J: Men might get things done a little quicker, people keep appointments with men and listen to them. Men are more respected than women. It's mostly men you have to deal with in the council. But this borough is full of amazing women, you know.

D: I don't think there's any need for men to be involved, not if you've got intelligent women. And someone who knows where to go. It's who you know - that's what matters. You must know your constitutional rights too. People realise, then 'she knows what she's all about'. If you just ask questions you won't get far.

At meetings, when men are there, do they tend to take the chair and do the talking?

D: Yes, they do really. We women still live in an age when we think men should act the major role.

J: At the street group I think we'd have got through more if we hadn't had minutes and that. Things went quickly by word of mouth. Minutes are a waste of time. It depends what you learned at school. But lots of women in our group didn't know what you were talking about if you talked about minutes. I think now that action speaks louder than words. I wouldn't bother with it.

Will your husband stay at home while you go out to meetings?

D: Yes, he will. And help me with writing letters. But he doesn't do housework. No. That he doesn't do.

J: That's a difference. My husband won't support me when I get involved, he thinks it's a waste of time.

Does change have to come first in the home, if women are to get free to be involved outside?

D: Yes. Men should realise it is no longer a woman's duty to run a house. Yes. It should be teamwork. Men really have to experience how things are for you, if they are going to understand.

I often walk my child to school in the rain. I'd tell him how
terrible it was. Then he did it one day - just once. It was
enough. He said, 'I don't know how you do it.' After that, he
knew. Now, I push off early on a Saturday morning and when he
wakes up I've gone, and he has the kids to look after. When I come
back he's tired out. Now he'll help more, because he knows.

J: I walked out last year for a week when things were very bad.
I went to the Women's Centre. Straight away my husband took the
child to his mother - the very next morning. And made an arrange-
ment, the next week, if I didn't come back, to share with another
woman who had a kid and would look after Stephen.

He straight away looked to another woman to cope with his problem?

J: Yes. Even if I'm ill, he won't take a day off work to look
after Stephen or me.

Once you get involved outside the house, do things change inside?

D: Yes. If you can be involved in something and care enough
about it, then your husband will have to act the role of mum and dad
sometimes. My husband has respected me a lot since then.   But it
depends on the man. Some would say, 'She's become too domineering
for me.' That would be it.

*That sounds as if, to be the sort of women we can respect, we
have to become the sort of women that men don't like. Do we have
to choose?*

D: Some men don't mind it.

J: Anyway you can change. You can be domineering one evening
and the next day you can be meek and mild with him. We have to be
devious to be women. I don't like it, but we do.

*Do men have such power over us that we have to split ourselves
like that?*

D: They tend not to realise we're human beings. They think of us
as mums to wash and scrub and clean, and don't consider we've got
minds. I try to stay attractive. I try to spend at least one hour
a day on myself. I think a woman should try to do that - one hour to
herself every day - it would lift your morale.

J: I keep saying I'm going to do that. But at six in the evening I find I haven't even brushed my hair some days.

Do men try and stay attractive for women?

J: Only for their work. For people outside.

*Do you think a woman's experience, like being pregnant and
bringing up children, being in bad housing all day, can make her
stronger than a man for some things?*

D: Yes. For me.

J: And look at the women at Women's Aid. Some of them have had
to defend themselves against men, protect themselves with knives.
After what they've been through - now they can fight.

How did your confidence grow?

D: It was having nowhere to live. That was the first thing.
Life was a real burden. Being pregnant and ill. We had this tri-
bunal. They all asked my husband the questions. They ignored me.
As though I didn't exist. And then I said, 'Gentlemen, excuse me.
No one has asked me how I feel about it. I don't want to go back
in that flat.' They were shocked. But they listened.

When I came to England I had very little confidence. In the
West Indies I was really sheltered by my family. I had no man in

those days. When I married, life was a burden. My husband, now, he
sees the difference in me. He says now I've lots of confidence.
If he is away at work and things happen, I don't say to myself,
'wait till he come home', I solve the problem myself.

J: Yes. Like when I found a dead rat in the cupboard the other
day. I didn't wait for Alan to come back. I just ripped the cupboard out of the wall myself and burned it.

D: Now I don't take no for an answer and I know I wouldn't fail.
I have one object now: not to fail. It works, if you are persistent. The important thing is: don't lose your self-respect.

How can you help women to get the confidence that you've got?

D: I'd get right in and help, and be on and on at that person
all the time.

J: If necessary I'd leave my house and go and live with them
and work alongside them.

D: You have to have a lot of patience and tolerance. People on
this estate have so many problems. When you have problems you need
someone to help you. You don't have the energy - but it's a slow
process. Some of us get depressed. We just can't be bothered.

Yet, when you ...

D: Yes. I was a rebel. In those days I was a rebel. Now I'm
a lady back again. You can't keep up being a rebel all the time.
But when it comes it - now I know I'll fight.

The second conversation I had was with Jan Kirk, who is married and
has four children. She too lives on a south London Council estate
and, like so many of us, has gone into work with children (in a
playgroup on the estate) as the only practicable complement to work
with children (at home).

Cynthia: *If Tom hadn't joined the tenants' association, would
you have done it on your own*?

I don't think I'd have been strong enough to go in without Tom at
the beginning, because he wouldn't have understood how I felt about
doing it. I know myself that if I don't understand something he's
doing, to me it seems stupid.

*So for some women, whose husbands don't get involved, it would be
more difficult than it was for you*?

Yes. From what I hear about it. When you start getting involved
you find you're not a cabbage any more. You've got a mind and can do
things. I don't think men like that idea. A lot of women won't do
it. They say it's the husband who pays the rent, it is his thing all
the time. Even if you ask people to join the tenants' association,
they say, I'll wait for my husband to come home and see if he says
I can join.'

I was like that a few years ago. Some women will go along with
anything the men say. At the beginning I did too, to be honest. But
as you go on you get to know - I'll argue now.

What changed you?

It was getting the tenants' association started. That is what
changed things for me.

What were things like before that?

In those days I had no confidence, not for that sort of thing.
At one time we were homeless. We were evicted. We went to live with

my parents. Then we went to a reception centre, and later to a
welfare flat.

What did you do about it?

It wasn't me. It was Tom. He was the one who went to see
people. And when we were being evicted from the flat above the pub
where Tom worked, he put up placards saying 'Landlord evicting
family with three kids'.

What did you feel about it?

Oh, I was just embarrassed. I didn't want anyone to know I lived
there. I wish I'd felt then what I do now. I'd have backed him.
I wouldn't have gone to the reception centre for one thing, I can
see now. You get pushed from pillar to post. I'd have stuck it
out in the pub till we were actually thrown out. I had never
squatted then - but I would now.

*Did getting involved outside make a difference to how things were
at home?*

Yes. At the time I wasn't working and being in all the time
doing nothing got on top of me. As I began to go out, things
indoors seemed more trivial. And my kids were all in school. Oh,
things are never like they used to be here. I let things go now.
It used to be well turned out, all clean.

Does Tom complain?

Oh no. It was always he who was the one to say 'leave it'.
It was me, I was just like that. I couldn't do anything before the
beds were made and the floors clean. But when your kids are little
you never sit down. And still you get nothing done. Later, I think,
you do organise better.

Does Tom do more about the house than most men?

No. He doesn't do a lot for the kids. I was always here,
wasn't I? He was a paraffin salesman, then a minicab driver, he
was never here. Now he's unemployed, he's about more.

*Would it have been impossible for you to get involved if the kids
had been younger?*

Yes. But it was not so much evening meetings I was doing, as
leafleting round the estate and collecting contributions. Two of
us, both women, used to collect for the whole estate. I don't know
now how we did it.

Do men in the tenants' association share that kind of work?

There are two or three who didn't mind doing it. Men on the
whole don't like it, though. Perhaps they think they're above it. Or
they're more shy of knocking on doors. I don't mind doing that.
And I met a lot of people through it.

*Do you think the experience of women, looking after a man and
kids and a house, makes them more suited to action on the estate or
in the street than a man is?*

It ought to. But women will moan and then not do anything about
it. More will come to a meeting than men, and they'll complain and
shout, but they won't do anything. They wouldn't hold back the rent
increases when we wanted to, they were afraid of everything.
They're scared all the time. 'My rent book's never had a stain on
it.' They were afraid that their transfer would be held up, or they
might be evicted. They don't see that they couldn't evict the whole
estate.

Is it women's lack of confidence?

It all boils down to power. They think that men have the power
and better education. It's words. Councillors and people use
words that lots of women don't understand. I don't understand
them either. But I know that often the people who use them don't
understand them either - and there's no need for them.

*Is it what their husbands think that stops women getting
involved?*

I don't know. I think Tom's realised I'm a human being since
I did this. He used to think I had no ideas and opinions of my
own. And you grow into it yourself and believe those things about
yourself, in the end. He never liked the idea of my going to work;
now he doesn't mind.

Are men useful in action over things like housing and children?

Yes. When a man's voice opens up in a group of women they all
listen - and the council take more notice of men, definitely. The
thing is, with women, with me too, when I'm here talking to you and
when I'm in the playgroup or in a meeting, wherever I am, half my
mind is over there with my parents, half with the kids. There are
so many things I'm thinking about all the time. When you go to a
meeting you don't put your full force into it. Half of you isn't
there. A man has only got to concentrate on that one thing. He
can put everything into it.

But when I'm at a meeting, by about ten o'clock I'm thinking,
'Are the kids in bed, I bet they're not and they'll be tired for
school in the morning.' I'm not listening to who is talking.

Up to a couple of years ago the children were my life. If I
left Roy with anyone so that I could go out I'd be thinking all
the time, 'Are the windows safely locked where he is?' So many
things go through my mind. When a man goes away from home and
from the kids, he forgets. He puts them out of his mind. It's
not like that for us.

What these conversations showed me, in fact what they showed all of
us as we talked, was how impossible it is for a woman to split off
her outward action from her domestic life and relationships. If she
gets involved in class struggle it drags her unwittingly onto a new
course as a woman, affects all that she is as a woman. Relationships
with husbands become tougher, more stringent - but also at best more
equal and respectful. Both Dorothy and Jan have gone from the
action they describe into work in a local playgroup - into communal
child care that is paid (however badly) and contrasts with the priva-
tised child care they continue to experience at home. In this new
work they are more aware than they would have been five years ago of
the woman's role they play in it, of the way the mothers they meet
relate to their own children or husbands, and of the authority
structures within the job. Even to take a part-time job at all, and
become part of the paid workforce, causes a shift in a woman's domestic experience, in the way we view a husband, and our housework.
'To abandon the home is already a form of struggle.' (6)

Women bring a totality, an all-or-nothing feeling to action. It
is something of which trade unions and political parties with their
hierarchies and agendas know little, and to which they can give
little. This totality is not just of the work day but of the whole

day, not just of wages but of feelings, not just of economics but of relationships. That women's action till now has been relatively weak and momentary, that it lacks the sanctions of large-scale organisation, everyone knows. But it has one great power - unexpectedness. Women's action is revolutionary because its nature is to cut across all the fossilised expectations of industrial negotiation and electoral politics; thus it is less easily bought off. It seems to me that we are trying, or have to try, to use these group strengths and sustain each other in action when the costs for us as individuals become too high.

Notes

1 'Knuckle', Lambeth and Southwark monthly paper, 1 January 1975. Thanks to Knuckle Collective for permission to reproduce.
2 These ideas have been put forward by many Marxist feminist writers, but for a very useful and succinct statement see Maria Rosa dalla Costa's 'The Power of Women and the Subversion of the Community', Bristol, Falling Wall Press, 1972. It has been an important step in women's consciousness to recognise the money value of their housework, but most women feel that merely to ask for payment, and perhaps get it, would confirm them in their housebound and 'inferior' role - the last thing they want.
3 I leave aside here woman's other economic role as a reserve workforce.
4 Elizabeth Wilson, 'Women and the Welfare State', 'Red Rag' pamphlet no. 2, 1974.
5 Mala Dhondy, Asian women strike, in 'All Work and no Pay', W. Edmond and S. Fleming, eds, Bristol, Falling Wall Press, 1975.
6 dalla Costa, op.cit.

8 Mothers in action, 1967-75

Shirley Frost

GETTING STARTED, 1967-8

When we first started Mothers in Action in 1967, there were few or no pressure groups run by non-professionals. Perhaps that is why so many people were patronising, to the point of being insulting. The field, you see, had been monopolised by well-meaning social workers for so long that many organisations resented our sudden appearance on the scene. In those days it was customary for single mothers (unmarried they were called) to be referred automatically to Moral Welfare Workers employed by the Church of England or, in the case of Roman Catholics, to the Crusade of Rescue - the same thing under a different hat. The history of this goes back to the nineteenth-century movement to reform prostitutes; in their eyes, presumably, any woman in the single state who bore a child needed to repent of her sins. Added to this was the later view that by definition such a woman was in need of psychiatric help - indeed many women were admitted to mental institutions by relatives, and two such women in their sixties, apparently quite normal, were released from institutions in 1974. This view is very much part and parcel of social work teaching with its pseudo-psychoanalytical theories. Particular hostility has always been reserved by society for the poor, and, of course, unsupported women and children figured largely amongst the inmates of the poorhouses and workhouses.

Initially we were five single mothers who came to know each other through the National Council for the Unmarried Mother and her Child (now One-Parent Families). We all shared, it seems, the belief that society was treating us unjustly, although individually our experiences had been quite different. So an organisation was set up at our first meeting in Wimbledon with specific campaigning objectives. We knew that one person alone could not make much impact but we felt that by asking other members to join us we would become strong enough for people to take notice. So what was our case?

We were, then, principally interested in day care for children of all ages, tax concessions, provision of housing, and reform of the laws of inheritance in relation to 'illegitimate' children who could not, at that time, inherit from their parents unless named in a will. We also wanted maintenance arrangements charged so that maintenance

71

and affiliation payments would be awarded on the basis of (the father's) ability to pay, rather than some arbitrary sum, as was then the case.

We also undertook to disseminate information so that people would be in a better position to help themselves. But first of all we had to get the information - no easy task in those days. Only three weeks after our first meeting we were approached by World in Action, with a view to doing a programme. We were naturally a bit 'green' and it became obvious to us in the course of filming that they were not really interested in our case as such but whether we would make good television. It is possible to treat a subject seriously without sacrificing anything to visual effect; in our case (in our opinion), that was hardly attempted and at the end we would have been quite happy if the interviewer, the producer and the camera crew had fallen down the nearest manhole. Our publicity officer, Junida, was a law student at the time and she had been trying to persuade various people to support a change in the Maintenance Orders Act. Finally it was Quintin Hogg who took her up on this, and after asking her to write out a report on the whole matter, had, without notifying her, presented a Private Member's Bill which was eventually passed. So he was roped into the World in Action programme because he was a personality; we resented the implication that we were not interesting enough by ourselves. The film crew seemed overawed by him - but we were not. When he was leaving he said, 'Poor things' - we were furious, pity was the last thing we wanted! It was early experiences like this that determined many of our later attitudes. We learned to be cynical.

We refused to have any social workers or other 'professionals' as full members; we did not want them to be in a position to say what we should or should not do. Second, we refused to provide mothers as 'media fodder' - if someone wanted an interview we offered ourselves to talk about our objectives. In addition, we refused any interviews about sex, marriage or birth control because we knew that they were intended to titillate or shock, not to inform. The other alternative was the 'sob story' approach and we did not like that either. Journalists and TV producers frequently told us we were 'unco-operative'.

An article in 'The Times' quickly followed the TV programme (which we have been trying to live down ever since) and the floodgates opened. Letters poured in from all over the country, even from abroad, and surprisingly many were from divorced, deserted and separated women who pointedly referred to the meaningless of a wedding ring. So we changed our brief to one of 'unsupported' mothers. We got the cranky letters too but we had a good laugh and put them in our 'odd letters' file. After the 'Times' article, Junida had been put under pressure from her family in Malaya because of the publicity, and also the powers-that-be at the Middle Temple. Her conduct, they said, was unbecoming to a future barrister. Anyway, the Maintenance Orders (Amendments) Bill went through Parliament and we put the first notch on our belts. Some will say it was on the cards anyway, but it is absolutely clear that the initiative of one woman who was personally affected had succeeded where other well-meaning organisations and individuals had failed.

We felt that whilst we could offer a national campaigning base,

something more locally based was also necessary, so that mothers
could meet together for support and to deal with local issues. In
all, we helped to set up twenty-two local groups, which involved a
great deal of time, patience and paperwork. But we over-estimated
the support we would get for the actual campaigns. Many mothers did
not share our confidence and could not see beyond their own personal
problems. For instance, a mother who had not had any housing problems (and this was very rare) could not see why she should be expected to support a campaign on housing and believed that people
became homeless because they were irresponsible. We were opposed
to this attitude because we knew that it was only by well-organised
collective action that any change could occur. The causes had to be
attacked, not the symptoms. Otherwise, the same symptoms would
occur again and again, and this was demonstrated by the contents
of the numerous letters we received, some of which practically
duplicated each other. We quickly realised the extent to which these
women suffered years of poverty, humiliation and rejection.

    In order to let members know what we were doing, we sent out a
newsletter several times a year. This was often typed surrepti-
tiously at work in our lunch hours and run-off on borrowed dupli-
cators, which involved us in trailing around various parts of north
London with suitcases of duplicating paper, often with a young child
in tow who kept putting fingers in impossible places as the frantic
churning of the duplicator exercised its particular capacity to
fascinate. We also wrote up a number of simple fact-sheets which we
sent out for a nominal sum of money.

National Council for the Unmarried Mother and her Child

What of the NCUMC in all this? Although their director had been
instrumental in bringing us together in the first place, we carefully avoided an ongoing association with them because we did not
want the shadow of patronage hanging over us. We did not want to
create the impression that we were just another bunch of do-gooders,
who wanted only to placate instead of to respond positively to the
experiences that people were having. Either we would do it on our
own merits or not at all. Often it was the latter. The Children's
Officer for Nottingham, for instance, refused to answer a circular
about day nurseries because he was 'getting too many of these types
of enquiries and it was not on headed paper'!

CONFRONTATION, 1968-9

Our first campaign was on day-care for the under-fives, and we soon
learned how important it was to have data, the right sort of data,
to support our case. A chance contact at the National Society for
Children's Nurseries (now amalgamated with Early Childhood Education) provided us with a copy of a research project on local authority day nursery provision some years earlier. On the basis of this
we wrote to the Minister of Health and asked all our members to send
the same letter. The reply was both inappropriate and unacceptable,
so as he was my MP (Kenneth Robinson), I got on the end of his

monthly advice session in the constituency at Camden Town Hall.
He was furious and politely tried to throw me out - 'because I
don't discuss Ministerial matters in this situation'. I stuck to
my guns and pointed out his erroneous thinking. He suggested that
we write in and ask to send a delegation to see him to discuss the
matter properly. We did and were refused. But the upshot of all
this was that within a few months a circular was issued which
asked local authorities to submit information about day care needs,
while reassuring them that they did not need to do any research.
The wording of the circular (37/68) started, 'in view of enquiries
and representations' - I presume this was referring to us. We
were mildly pleased; at least we had managed to pierce their carefully erected smoke-screen. When we rang the Ministry and asked
for a copy of the circular, we were told that 'this is not meant
for the public'. We pointed out that we had a special reason for
wanting it as we believed that we probably had been instrumental in
its going out. The voice at the end of the telephone said, 'Oh no,
that can't be possible!'

What we needed at that time was access to a good library and someone to take the children off our hands whilst we searched for the
information we needed. We never got that and, of course, it made
it very difficult for us to articulate our demands in a precise way.
There were professionals who could have helped us but as we gave
them the brush-off as far as running the organisation was concerned, we could not really expect them to help us with this.
There were plenty of people who wanted to pick our brains in order
to publish trendy articles. We wanted to be helped in our way, but
this was something that people rarely accepted. As far as we were
concerned, if you were not for us you were against us.

Paper-bound

To make matters worse, our mail now included a sizeable proportion
of letters from social workers wanting advice. This was adding
insult to injury. Not only were we struggling to deal with desperate letters from people who had already been to social workers and
found them inadequate to the situation, we were now expected to 'wet
nurse' the social workers as well. Our hostility to social workers
really originated in this general climate of ineptitude. We had to
find out the hard way how to get hold of the information that people
wanted and we did not see why social workers should not do the same.
Of course, the profession has taken steps to improve its track
record, but it is only through grass-roots organisations like
Mothers in Action that any attempt has been made at all.

Our absorption with answering between 100 and 200 letters a week
meant that we were not continuing with our campaigns. By 1970 we
had more or less come to a halt, paper-bound. In addition, our
local groups were not doing well. Their expectations of what we
could do without their support were somewhat unrealistic. Suffice
it to say that there were misunderstandings, disappointments and
disillusion. By the end of 1971 we had decided that drastic steps
were needed and a chance remark by Frank Field, Director of the
Child Poverty Action Group, led us to make an application for funds,

which was successful. So at least we got our office and could employ
someone to carry out routine tasks, which was necessary because it
is difficult for lone parents to maintain continuity in this kind of
all-embracing endeavour because of their substantial domestic commitments. We told our members that we could not continue to service
them and run campaigns, and we preferred to run campaigns as we
felt this would be the most effective way of spending resources and
would benefit more people.

TARGETS

So we abandoned formal membership and spent the next twelve months
in sorting ourselves out. There were new problems to be faced now;
the responsibility of the office and the people who worked there.
We set up several working groups to establish a coherent basis from
which to operate, but few people came forward so we had to do the
work ourselves, which meant that our progress was painfully slow.
By 1973 we had decided to re-orientate ourselves once again. We
chose four major areas of work which we felt covered common areas
of difficulty in the lives of all one-parent families, regardless
of their status. These were housing, day care, incomes, education
and employment opportunities. We called this 'Target - better
living standards for one-parent families', and we sent out a free
monthly bulletin elaborating on these four topics. Four of us took
responsibility for co-ordinating campaigns, and we promised ourselves that we would initiate a new campaign four times a year;
we almost managed to keep to this target! We tried to involve
other parents in what we were doing by asking them to write in
specifically and send us local newspaper cuttings, for example. By
now, for reasons which I am not really clear about, many people
seemed to be under the impression that Mothers in Action was a huge
organisation, and we left it that way when it seemed an advantage.
In fact, there were never more than ten active members of the organising committee at any one time. When people rang up and asked
for the publications department we would yell out to Rita, sitting
two desks away, in our cramped office. But often it was also a
strain because people's expectations of what we could achieve were
unrealistic. Some found it difficult to believe, for instance, that
we were not all drawing a salary of at least £2,000 a year. In fact,
none of us got paid, except for expenses like babysitting or fares to
the office, sometimes to demonstrations as well!

THEORY AND PRACTICE, 1971-2

In addition to the thousands of women bringing up families single-
handed there were (then) an unspecified number of men doing the
same. They had largely remained invisible until Gingerbread started
up in 1970. One of the problems of looking at lone parents as a
group is that there is a hierarchy of deservedness among them which
has been largely internalised. Widows are at the top as the most
deserving, and single mothers and prisoners' wives are at the bottom.
Not only does the state and its institutions operate this scale, but

the parents themselves do too, creating hostility and competition between them. This has to some extent been mitigated by having an umbrella title such as 'One-parent families', instead of picking people off by referring to the particular social situation which has contributed to their status.

Many previously married parents, for instance, preferred not to work with us because they imagined that our unmarried status would reflect badly on them, or felt that our attitudes were too uncompromising. They felt that to 'demand' anything was the wrong way of going about any attempt to improve the position of lone parents. Gingerbread, for instance, always emphasised that they worked with social services rather than against them. Our attitude, on the other hand, was always 'What social services?' We had learned from bitter experience that polite letters nearly always resulted in equally polite but (practically) useless replies. This was before the publication of the Finer Report (on one-parent families) and the battery of evidence and statistics to substantiate our claims, if not demands. Even now, the government still gives out the equivalent of polite replies when asked about its intentions towards the implementation of the major parts of the Report. But finally, it was Gingerbread in 1974 that organised a march to Parliament to protest about the government's inactivity. I often wonder if any of them were the same people who insisted that we were too militant. Gingerbread had concentrated on groups for social contact, and taking to the streets was evidence of growing anger from a previously unexpected quarter. The scene in the House of Commons, when many parents had been refused entry to see their MPs after having travelled all day with children, had to be seen to be believed. The MPs who well-meaningly offered themselves to address parents in a committee room were told to sit down and listen, and I was for one full of admiration for the ordinary parents who had probably never spoken in public in their lives before, and who told in vivid terms just what it meant to be a one-parent family in 1975. The fact that MPs had just given themselves a pay rise only added fuel to the fire. I can say in all honesty that it was worth waiting eight years to see MPs confronted with their own complacency. The fact that these MPs were part of the all-party committee formed to put pressure on the government escaped most people's notice. The act of protest was a symbolic one, a climax to years of grinding poverty and unremitting humiliation.

So Gingerbread had been first and foremost a socially-orientated organisation and we had not. We had taken to getting our name put on the list of women's groups, rather than 'help' groups, in magazine articles. We would have been prepared to work with male lone parents but as a number of them had openly attacked our feminist image we did not pursue the matter. We always had, in addition, a loose sort of socialist perspective and towards the end we often put this forward as our label when pressed for information. The objectives of Mothers in Action, Gingerbread and One-Parent Families are not all that different - but the individual perspectives and the ways that they are pursued do vary somewhat.

The very heart of the one-parent family situation is the idea of the division of labour between the man and the woman (in the latter case, unpaid), and similarly the division between work outside and

inside the home, the latter including the care of children. Not
surprisingly it was, in the end, the Women's Liberation Movement
that gave us the most concrete support. But then I would have been
surprised if this had not been so. It just took time to material-
ise.   We had developed a set of practical objectives which had
perhaps an unconsciously feminist base. But we had not, for
instance, developed a theoretical approach, at least not on paper,
although we had discussed endlessly the theory of what we were
doing. We just did not have the confidence to put it on paper.
We felt that some things were better left unsaid if we wanted to
get any support at all. We were also conscious of the fact that
many lone parents themselves, while agreeing with the validity of
our objectives, would not agree with the manner in which we came
to our conclusions. We felt that in any case this did not matter;
the objectives would stand or fall on their own merits. To get
caught up in an ideological argument which by itself would not do
anything to improve the position of lone parents within society
would be tantamount to self-indulgence. We were interested in the
means to self-improvement, not the idea of the self-improvement
itself, which could easily degenerate into a kind of paternalism.
Although we were for a long time suspicious even of the women's
movement, feeling that they could not appreciate the nature of our
experiences, it was clear later on that the analysis of women's
oppression was a powerful base on which to balance our particular
set of objectives, precisely because it pinpointed the role of the
family in serving the interests of an economic system in which women
were second-class citizens. We saw male lone parents as experiencing for the first time the dual role that women play as a matter of
course - that of being a breadwinner and a homemaker in a society
in which it is increasingly common for mothers to work.

FRUSTRATION, 1969

A lot of our time over the last few years has been spent on dealing
with housing problems, and homelessness principally. In the end,
all we could do was to tell people to squat and give them a book
telling them how to do it. If the housing situation had been bad
before, now it was terrible. But squatting is not usually an ideal
life for people with children unless they are with a group of people
who will be supportive and at least share some of the work of looking
after children. For some parents, this works out better than expected. They frequently balk at the idea of squatting, feeling it to
be a big come-down. But when, and if, they are eventually rehoused
in a nice new council flat, they can then find that this is a trap.
They cannot afford to pay for the central heating, they cannot go
out socially, and the neighbours complain about the children making
a noise. On the other hand, for most parents, the only prospect of
rehousing is the local authority. We came to understand that local
authorities frequently displayed the most appalling insensitivity
and bureaucracy. I spent hours and hours on the telephone each week
trying to get local authorities to take positive action to help homeless families, and frequently these authorities were obstructive and/
or indifferent. I soon took to cutting through their thick skins

with a few forcefully delivered insults, which is where I got a reputation for being 'rude', although it is interesting to note that what is considered rude in the south of England is considered 'plain speaking' in the north, where I was brought up.

Women with violent husbands also phoned several times a week, and all I could usually do was to suggest they contact the usual agencies for various kinds of help. I rang up a few people to see if I could draw together a useful body of information, but I got nowhere. The marriage guidance council wanted to send me someone to talk about group co-ordinators, and a solicitor, who had been recommended to me by a civil liberties organisation, suggested that such women should join a tenants' association. Solicitors usually told them to leave their husbands, but of course there was nowhere to go.

PUTTING IT ON PAPER, 1974-5

During 1974 and 1975 we concentrated very hard on setting out on paper the ways in which we thought help should be given to one-parent families. We managed to produce papers on maternity leave and job security; day care for the under-fives and for school-age children; facilities needed for school-age mothers, and so on. We had intended to produce a paper on housing dealing with the function of architecture and planning in structuring family size. We felt we needed some 'experts' for this, and although we tried various sources no one was interested. We were interested to explore possible alternatives to the standardised nuclear family living unit, which is so often unbearably isolating to one-parent families. We wanted to see whether something like the extended family could be created from social groups who were not necessarily related to each other, and to see what sort of housing would lend itself to shared activities both within and between such groups. Another area we turned out minds to was education. We wanted to take one area and make a careful study of the educational opportunities, of the women who lived in the area and their needs, and whether there was any lack of provision, for whatever reason. We were also interested in investigating how, for instance, the acquisition of skills, education and provision of child-care facilities could be combined in one scheme. We applied to a number of trusts for funds to do the work because our grant had run its course, but were refused.

We also spent a lot of time discussing the Children Bill. This was a Bill which arose originally out of the Houghton Committee on Adoption. The Bill was expanded to include clauses on children in care, cruelty, and so on. It was labelled 'the Children's Charter' but we considered it anything but that. In fact we saw it as highly reactionary for the following reasons - it contained the statutory means for transferring children from one family situation to another (more preferred) one, without in any way modifying the situation which had brought about a need to consider such an action in the first place. We saw the effect of the Bill as one of providing the state with further intervention powers in relation to the family, intervention designed to preserve bourgeois ideology disguised as a concern for the rights of the children. The clauses would, in effect, relate mainly to one-parent families - for instance, instant consent to adoption rather than a three-month probationary period, a pilot scheme to pay allowances to adopters, compulsory notification of intent to remove a child from (voluntary) care, the right of foster parents to apply for adoption after a specified number of years, the right of courts to dispense with parents' permission for adoption to take place after a specified number of years in care, and so on. The factors which put lone parents fairly and squarely in the centre of this Bill are as follows - the children of lone parents account for a significant proportion of children in care (these would be the foster children referred to in the Bill); and single mothers provide the majority of children (especially babies) available for adoption. The problem is that the handicaps under which lone parents bring up their children are not considered, so the Bill was seen by us as an expediency, a cheap way out of a situation which had been awaiting a solution for many years. While not all admissions to care, adoptions and cases of neglect and cruelty can be accounted for by bad housing conditions, poverty of income and experience, lack of social services, etc., it is clear (at any rate to us) that lone parents as a group do not care less for their children than other parents. We would therefore look for environmental reasons for the disproportionate numbers who appear in the statistics. By arguing against the Children Bill it looks as if we were insensitive to the needs of children, but this is an incorrect assumption; it is precisely because we were sensitive to their needs that we drew attention to the injustice of providing a means for children to be removed from their families without balancing this with provision for them to remain there. We felt that if children had the right to be removed from families where their welfare was clearly going to be a long-term risk, they also had the right to remain in their families if their parents showed concern for them, but lacked the means to express it. There is at work, mostly unseen, the ideological view that a one-parent family is not a 'proper' family; if this is so, we would point out that if society were organised differently one would not even have to think about such things. Children would grow up in social groups large enough to provide a variety of adult models and relationships as a matter of course, and the presence or otherwise of their biological parents would cease to have the pathological importance it has today. They would also be a lot healthier emotionally.

Our views on day care provision for children in one-parent families were that children should not be segregated but cared for within a general framework of care for all children. We suggested, among other things, that there should be liaison between local authority departments and recipients of the services, and at national level between the various ministries concerned. There is evidence that this is now happening but, of course, the cuts in spending have provided the excuse needed not to do anything concrete. But even this does not mean that one should not continue to work at breaking down barriers between concerns. In particular, we suggested that present provisions should be extended to include an educational or care aspect as the case may be, and that, ideally, each

neighbourhood should have its own children's care centre which
would have a framework of community involvement and management, and
which would also meet the needs of parents for social contact, etc.
There are a few schemes like this and they are not without their
problems, but it is through projects like this that one can demonstrate what is possible. We found this a particularly exciting
idea for women and children generally, now that families have been
split up into smaller and smaller units through redevelopment, etc.
One fact is certain, with smaller families as a permanent feature of
our society in the future, we must recognise that children are, as
a result, deprived of important emotional and social experiences
and we must find ways to compensate them for this. People who
protest about the effects of day care provision in encouraging
mothers to work just do not know the facts, either about working
mothers or the contemporary needs of children.

School-age children are a particularly neglected group, especially between the ages of five and eleven.   They no longer fascinate
the students of early childhood development, and they do not, on
the whole, threaten to turn us upside down as teenagers are imagined
to do. Nevertheless, they are very much a growing, developing
entity and it is during this period that they consolidate their
early learning experiences and move towards puberty. Since they
are imaginative, physically active and socially curious, they do
not require the same close physical supervision as the under-fives.
They should have a framework that provides for all their diverse
needs to be met - without appearing to cramp them but, at the same
time, enabling them to ask for help if it is wanted. In the past,
this has been served by the 'mother-at-home' model'; an ever-open
back door and tolerance of noise and mess. For children with
parents at work, no garden and hostile adults all around them,
something is urgently required so that their development can take
place unhindered. For this reason we spent some time working with
the Fair Play for Children campaign, urging that facilities for care
and play be brought together; but appreciation of the need for this
is slow, possibly non-existent.

It is common for the income of a couple to fall before and after
the birth of a child, starting with the first. For the unattached
woman this usually means she has to apply for Supplementary Benefit
because obviously maternity benefit (assuming she is eligible) is
rarely enough to live on. We felt that many women would prefer to
continue to receive their usual wages and have the security of being
able to return to work after a period of maternity leave. So we set
up what we called the Maternity Leave Campaign, which had six main
points based on the European agreement for maternity provisions.
The Tory government just fobbed us off. The Labour government
finally, after a number of prompts, made concessions in the Employment Protection Bill, which was a start although it did not go nearly
far enough. People thought we were mad to ask for a time-off clause
for nursing mothers, but a little later the Department of Health produced a report emphasising the importance of breast-milk and breast-
feeding for the physical and emotional health of children. We would
not want anyone to be forced to breast-feed against their will, but
a choice should be available, even if you are working. It is up to
working women everywhere to improve on the minimal provisions made,
to ensure that pregnancy does not mean economic dependency.

CONCLUSIONS

By the time the reader sees this, Mothers in Action will no longer exist. This was an on-the-spot decision which came almost exactly eight years after its beginning. Eight years of continual effort and struggle is immensely exhausting, and our own personal lives had to a large extent taken a back seat. We thought that our reserves of energy had run out and needed replenishing while we did something completely different for a time. We also felt that, where before we had needed an office, this very office now threatened to swamp us. It had supported us through periods of self-examination and reorganisation but now it had taken on a life of its own, which was almost parasitic. We wanted time to reflect, to see how our ideas would change people's attitudes. There were many other organisations doing things which, to some extent, overlapped, so that we did not feel we were indispensable.

So we packed up the letters, the reports, the books representing eight years of work and put them into storage, where they will stay so that we can refer to them in order to write our book. When we started out, we said to each other, 'We're making history'; we were very conscious of that and kept a copy of everything we had published so that we could write our own history.

This brief account obviously cannot hope to convey everything that happened. Hardly a day went by without some significant event. But what I have tried to do is to indicate the main aspects we were concerned about, and to give an idea of our successes and failures. I think perhaps the most generalised single achievement was to overturn the traditional stereotype of the undeserving, 'unmarried' mother, who at best was entitled to pity and not much else. It was worth it just for that alone.

9A **Gingerbread**
The challenge of self-help

Janet Hadley

In the mid-sixties, after twenty years of the bureaucracy of the welfare state, an increasing number of sections of the community began to organise in a new way to confront the social definitions which were imposed upon them by the state. Black people gave a lead in challenging the hypocritical hand-wringing of the Race Relations Acts, and refused any longer to accept the racist liberal definitions of blacks as passive victims to whom the host society must learn to be 'nice'. Gay men and women utterly rejected the concept of homosexuality as a 'sickness' and announced that they were very proud to be gay. Whole working-class communities organised to devastate Town Hall planners' expectations that motorways could be built over homes and whole areas rased to the ground without a murmur. Social security claimants militantly defended their rights to welfare. Everywhere isolation was breaking down. Against this background, a small number of one-parent families got together, sensing that no one who had not experienced bringing up a child alone could be as helpful to another lone parent as someone who had lived with the problems on a daily basis. The feeling was, 'To hell with the experts, with the social workers and shrinks - we are the experts - we have to live it every day.' And such a view has been confirmed time and again by newcomers to Gingerbread, the self-help association for one-parent families, exclaiming with relief:

> It felt so good to feel that people were at last on the same wavelength with me and could really understand what it was I was talking about - married friends and neighbours, my parents, the social worker, however sympathetic they are, they just can't know what it is really like.

I do not want to recite here the innumerable problems facing one-parent families. Anyone who wishes to know that in detail can find official information between the covers of the Finer Committee Report on One-Parent Families, now gathering dust in the archives of Whitehall with hardly any of its 230 recommendations implemented. But there are a few facts which readers must understand; more and more people will at some time in their lives be part of a one-parent family, and find out what it is like living in a society designed exclusively for the nuclear two-parent family. At any one moment, one out of every ten families with dependent children have only one

parent to look after them, and the total number of children is
more than a million, about as many as the population of a city
such as Birmingham.

Divorced or separated women are the largest group of single
parents, widows make up the next largest, and single, never-
married mothers are the smallest group. Five out of six lone
parents are women, but there is a growing number of fathers
caring alone for their children.

Much of the hardship facing lone parents and children is directly
related to the economic exploitation of women and to the fact that
women in general and mothers in particular are still treated as if
they were economically and socially dependent on men. Day-care
provisions for working parents are virtually non-existent and where
they do exist are usually inflexible and often expensive. The
average income of one-parent families is under half of that of two-
parent families' average income. A great many one-parent families
have to depend on Supplementary Benefit. Housing is a nightmare -
many lone parents are homeless or having to share overcrowded and
often substandard accommodation at punitive rents. Finally the
legal system, both the laws and the courts, are experienced as a
bewildering, absurd machine, perfectly designed to foster as much
bitterness and frustration as possible among people trying to
extricate themselves from their marriages.

Faced with an intractable problem of finding somewhere for herself
and her two small boys to live, with the Social Services Department
threatening to take the children into care if nowhere adequate
could be found, a lone mother feels embattled and desperately isolated. Just such a mother wrote to a Sunday newspaper, setting out
her own difficulties and suggesting that if there was anyone out
there in the same boat, she would like to join up to organise for a
better deal for one-parent families. A flood of 300 letters came in
from all over the country, and in January 1970 Gingerbread began, to
'ginger' the government for more 'bread' (money) for one-parent
families.

Breaking down the long isolation was euphoric and released a wave
of energy - people in the London area met and tried to organise to
support and help each other. They wrote to people in the provinces
to put them in touch with other lone parents near by. Because housing was a problem which had been mentioned in so many letters, a
housing register was started, giving advice about rights, and sometimes arranging for people to share their homes with others. The
service was run by a lone mother who rapidly acquired a formidable
command of welfare rights which, combined with an exceptional sensitivity, enabled her to correspond warmly and in a confidence-
giving way, setting out for people the options they might have in
dealing with their own problems.

Gingerbread has expanded enormously. In January 1972 it won a
grant and free office accommodation from the Joseph Rowntree Social
Service Trust. By April 1972, thirty-five local self-help groups
were running, many of them based on contacts made initially as a
result of the response to the newspaper letter. Three years later
there were 150 groups and in the last year, 1975, more than two

groups a week have started up throughout Wales, Scotland, Northern
Ireland and England. Soon there will be over 300.

The groups are open to anyone who brings up children alone.
They hold regular meetings and arrange social activities for parents
and children, as well as running second-hand clothing and toy
pools and arranging baby-sitting. Fund-raising depends on the
usual jumble sales, but there is no subscription payable to
Gingerbread (which is perhaps unique in an organisation of such a
size - nationally there are 25,000 members). Although the local
group and its activity remains the core of the association, there
is a flourishing pen-friend scheme, run from the national office,
for those who live too far from a group to participate. There is
also a thriving magazine, 'Ginger', which comes out six times a year.

The association also runs, through its national office which is
staffed by six people, an advice service for lone parents, writing
and telephoning to give information about welfare rights and other
matters. Leaflets are also available on topics such as social security, eviction and family law, all designed to demystify the administration as much as possible. For example, warnings are given in
the eviction leaflet about how to counter the local authority's possible excuses for not taking action when you become homeless, such
as the 'Haven't you any friends or relatives you could stay with for
a while till we get something sorted out?' trap. It is, however,
essential to understand that advice, information and encouragement
given by Gingerbread is not given to 'clients' or 'cases'. 'Client',
with its implications of dependence and inequality is regarded by
Gingerbread as a dirty word.

As the organisation has consolidated and developed it has become
increasingly important as a focus for political pressure at a
national level. Through struggle, members acting together have
become quite militant about the lack of government action to help
them, and this anger culminated in an unforgettable demonstration
through London in July 1975. Five thousand parents and children,
the majority of whom had never taken part in any form of protest
before, marched to Parliament and ventilated their anger on bewildered MPs.

This national demonstration was important for two reasons. Many
MPs and government representatives were undoubtedly taken aback
at such vehemence and militancy from people they had been used to
consider as inarticulate and passively unfortunate - from a section
of the community about whom they could wax eloquent but to whom they
had never had to listen. And for many lone parents, both those
Gingerbread members who marched and those who didn't, as well as
those who had not yet heard of Gingerbread, the demonstration provided resounding evidence of the potential for lone parents who can
come together, with a dignified and positive identity, to fight
for the right to a decent standard of living for their children and
themselves. There need be no more isolation and hiding away in
shame, cringingly grateful for the humiliating pittance of Supplementary Benefit, simply because they had 'made a mess of their
marriages'. Now, instead of having to mumble an explanation of
'one-parent families' when strangers asked, 'Gingerbread, what on
earth is that?', lone parents heard people saying, 'Yes, I've heard
of that, you fight for one-parent families.'

Many people whose children are now grown up and who had to struggle to bring them up without the support of other lone parents, often being made to feel that they and their children were social pariahs in the community, say how much they wish there had been a Gingerbread for them. But although many members now do get help and support from their local group, some will acknowledge that at first, when, for whatever reason, their marriages broke up, they could not have even contemplated approaching Gingerbread, the daily problems were too overwhelming and they were too depressed to have been able to face even a group of people who had lived through similar hells to their own.

Gingerbread members tend to be mainly divorced and separated men and women; widows and widowers are under-represented, and there are hardly any single mothers, especially teenage mothers. The class background of the groups varies from place to place. In working-class areas, the groups are mainly working class, but a working-class mother in the lusher rural areas of the Home Counties may find little in common with the preoccupations of her local group; and apart from some of the south London groups, it seems that black lone parents can be counted in tens amongst the Gingerbread members.

Certainly, the association's image tends to be middle class, though the bulk of the membership is not. This may be because the more prosperous parents are more able to give time and energy to participating in the association and to consider election as representatives and organisers at regional and national levels. Parallel to the domination of the middle class is the over-representation, proportionately, of lone fathers in leadership positions, in spite of the fact that the majority of members are women. (It is interesting to note the impression that Gingerbread does contain a higher ratio of lone fathers to lone mothers, compared to the national one-parent family picture.)

As it has developed, Gingerbread has been fairly conventional in the political (non-party) views it has put forward as a national group, and there has been little or no questioning of the real value of pressure-group tactics through the 'usual channels'; lobbies, writing to MPs and local councillors and faith in 'rational persuasion' are the order of the day, although there is very real frustration at the slowness of these methods.

I have been dealing with the characteristics of Gingerbread and its members - in spite of the limitations which I feel the organisation has, there is one key issue which is much misunderstood and which I want to look at in more detail - the idea of self-help.

Self-help is a notion which the training of many people in the 'caring professions' undervalues and deprecates to the point that many practising social workers are utterly disbelieving of its use and may even find it threatening. (This is a strong assertion, I know, but it is based on countless conversations with social workers, and even community workers, who express incredulity at the possibility that any of their 'cases' could themselves come together and organise a local Gingerbread.) Although the groups welcome and very often need the support of local welfare organisations (to help to find a place to meet, or provide the use of a typewriter and duplicator), Gingerbread encourages no one but a lone parent to found a new group. Thus social workers who inquire are asked if they themselves are lone parents, and, if not, they are politely rejected, with the suggestion that they leave it to the people they so often call 'my mothers' to make their own independent contact, and to whom will be given all the help and information needed to form and sustain a group. Another widely held view is that Gingerbread is a welfare agency which can be used as a dumping-ground for 'difficult clients', with expectations of miracle solutions which no group can sustain. Self-help will always be limited to the extent that the people involved, in this case lone parents, all have their own families to care for, possibly in addition to jobs; there is only so much time they can give to the specific problems of other individuals in the group. And self-help means give and take, even if the give is not simultaneous with the take.

But self-help in the group can achieve a great deal, both for members and for other lone parents in the area. More and more groups are expanding their activities to undertake welfare rights work, and run play-schemes for their children in the holidays and after-school hours. Some are making contact with local women's refuges, and out of these activities comes more political action at local levels.

Gingerbread can never be a sanctuary from the world, but as long as one-parent families suffer from discrimination, economically or socially, there will be a need for it to act as a raft, where parents and children can catch their breath. Its value was summed up recently by one lone mother, who said:

> I used to feel so awkward admitting I was divorced, and my
> feeling of shame affected my children. Becoming active in
> Gingerbread, I found a confidence and talents which I didn't
> know I had, and I know I could cope on my own now. But what
> I've gained has made me even more determined to stick with my
> group and with Gingerbread, and fight till every single child in
> a one-parent family gets a fair deal.

Not quite what Dale Carnegie had in mind!

9B **Gingerbread**
Interview with a founder member
of a local group

Anne Harris

What does 'Gingerbread' mean to your group?
   The name, I think, is self-explanatory: 'Ginger', to ginger
up local authorities and Parliament, and 'bread', for more money,
of course. But I don't think that Gingerbread is basically just
for more money - we fight for better conditions all round.
   Our members include all one-parent families, whether the parent
is unmarried, divorced or widowed, or with the other partner in
prison, disabled or mentally ill. Gingerbread is literally for
everybody who is looking after a child on their own. There is also
the social side of Gingerbread, whereby you get to know people who
have similar problems in your area. Meeting somebody who is bringing up a child by himself/herself is good, because immediately you
have something in common.
   We try to help each other out in any way we can: for instance,
babysitting and looking after the children at weekends; or if someone goes into hospital, we try to take over.
   We have been going only for a year. We are really only just
getting organised in Camden, with different topics at each weekly
meeting. Speakers are invited - for instance, we hope to have child
psychologists to talk to us about child behaviour; about how we
should be bringing up our children, how we should face the problem
of telling our children why they belong to a one-parent family, and
how they have come to be in that position.
   How does the local organisation relate to the national committee?
   Well, not very well at the moment. Being a fairly new group, we
have to get to know each other first, before people are willing to
go along with what the national Gingerbread is trying to do. It's
very difficult to do everything - about six or seven people are
actually the mainstay of the group, and they cannot carry both the
social and the action sides of Gingerbread's work.
   At the moment we are not keeping up with the national activities
too well, although I myself have been on the regional committee and
been the regional committee representative at the national level -
but that just means me personally, and not the group. I hope now
that we have a committee, that Camden Gingerbread will take a much
more active interest in Gingerbread at a national level and follow
its policies. I think that we have been going long enough now to

start chasing up and pressurising our local MPs and councillors to support the Finer Report for more nursery and after-school care and for holiday facilities for working mums and dads, and also to press for housing facilities, making sure that one-parent families are accepted for housing in the same way as two-parent families.

Sometimes I think people feel very cut off from the national level of activity until suddenly something big happens that involves the whole of Gingerbread like the Day of Action demonstration in July 1975. When you get people going along to something like a demonstration, you do start to feel a part of a bigger body.

I think nowadays that most one-parent families have heard of Gingerbread through television, radio or magazines and, I hope, through local advertising. Whether they know exactly what Gingerbread does is another matter, but at least they know that Gingerbread is for one-parent families.

How did your local group start up?

When I was homeless, a social worker who was then helping me find a place also told me about Gingerbread and put me in touch with another girl in the area who was interested in starting a local branch, if she had some help.

So how did you get in contact with the other people?

We decided that we would have a meeting; so we put posters up at the local nurseries, the library and Health Centre. This took place on a Friday evening, and although it was a terrible night, pouring hard with rain and freezing, six people turned up.

Then we decided to have another meeting in two weeks' time, on a Sunday afternoon so that everyone could bring their children if need be. About twenty-five to thirty people came this time, with about sixty children, and the group took strength from there. I asked if anybody would like to follow the meeting up by a coffee evening when we could carry the discussion further, and some people volunteered their homes. After that, I phoned up the Gingerbread secretary and suggested that I start a local branch. And that's really how we got going.

Is that fairly typical of the way local groups, start up?

There are twenty-seven in the London Region, and I think basically that most of these did get started in the same way. Some of them have been going a lot longer and are very well established.

You said that social activity has been quite important in the early stages of your group.

Over the past year we have tried to organise a range of social activities, although in Camden it is very hard to arrange events to suit everyone as the area has such a diverse mixture of people. The sorts of activities we have tried to organise have been outings, picnics, bottle-parties and dinner-parties. The social activities are not just for the adults, they are also for the children as the children are, of course, very much a part of Gingerbread. They then come to realise that they are not the only ones who have just one parent.

Our local Gingerbread at times has been very depressing, as the hard core of the local group have worked very hard to organise events and then very few people have turned up. Many times over the last year I have wondered why I am bothering, but then something goes off very well and I feel that it is worth carrying on.

I think one of the reasons why some people only come along to, say, one meeting and no more is that they think that Gingerbread is immediately going to solve all their problems, e.g. baby-sitting or housing. What they do not realise is that Gingerbread is a self-help association and that it is only by all of us pulling our weight that we will ever get anywhere.

What other activities apart from the social ones do you thing you might organise?

At our Annual General Meeting we selected a committee; a secretary, chairman, group contact, treasurer and what we call 'welfare officers', which is an unfortunate name for these two people, but their task is to act upon the desperate phone calls we all too often receive. We often get phone calls, you see, saying that a man's wife/wife's husband has just left him or her. He or she is in a terrible state and has tried to commit suicide, or is just terribly depressed. These two people will be responsible for dropping everything and going over to talk it out with him or her.

They are also going to look at the reasons why people phone and make contact with us and just do not turn up. These welfare officers are going to go out and visit these people and also those who come once and then don't come again, to find out why not.

If we start in a small local way like this, then I think we can gradually get into the national side of Gingerbread, but we have to build the confidence of the members. We shall then want an action officer, that is a person who will really relate between Camden and the national level. Now that we have got a hard core who really want to make Gingerbread work in this area, I think we will succeed.

Do you think the problems that the single parent has to face are basically the same as those of the mother in a low-income two-parent family?

I think our problems are no different from those of a married couple of the lower wage bracket. The only difference is that there are two of them to fight, whereas with a one-parent family there is only the one who has to do it all. Outside of that I honestly do not think that families in the lower wage bracket have problems any different from ours. In fact they are probably worse off, in some ways, because one-parent families are meant to have priority nursery places whereas, of course, a two-parent family has no priority for these. So in fact they have a worse problem because the mother can never go out to work to get the extra money to pay for baby-sitters etc.

But certainly our problems are a lot worse than those of the married couples who can afford to pay for baby-sitters and for their children to go to private nurseries.

Do you think that it requires much more initiative being the only parent?

It depends of course on what sort of person you are. People like myself push it, whereas some will not. They will just sit back. But yes, I think you do have to take the initiative. And you have to realise that you are going to be doing it all yourself.

Can you say a little more about what you feel the group actually means to people in personal terms?

To start with, I think it gives them an evening out, because we can accommodate children at the meeting. It also stops the parents thinking that they are the only one-parent family in the world when they realise that lots of other people have the same problems and are fighting them single-handed. You also realise that in fact some are a lot worse off than yourself and that helps you to understand that you are not doing so badly after all.

Do you think it helps to give people confidence, then?

Oh yes, definitely. Two or three members have come and in fact have actually left Gingerbread, because in a way Gingerbread has done its work. For example, one was a very regular member. She hadn't been out for eighteen months since her husband left her and she had four children. She said that all she did was to work, cook, clean and collapse. When she started to come to Gingerbread she gradually got her confidence back - and then she went out and met outside friends. Then she did not come to Gingerbread any more. Well, she doesn't need to; Gingerbread has done all it needs to do, for it certainly has given her her confidence back.

Out of the group there are quite a few people who have made some very good friends. They have met people whom they would have chosen as friends even if they had not also had the common experience of being a one-parent family. I think you find that if you make a good friend, eventually you do also tell each other about what you have been through. And I think this is a really good relief; we all need this type of emotional let-out.

Do you think that there are differences between women and men in the group - do they have different experiences of being a one-parent family?

Most of the men - four or five of them - work, mainly because their children are older and at school. So this is one of the differences. Also it is easier for a man to get home help - although apparently it is meant to be open for women as well, I have not yet met a one-parent mum who has ever got home help. The Social Services Department - everybody - is much more understanding of the problems of lone fathers, in fact. If there is nobody to collect their children from school, for instance, somehow or other social services will arrange it; whereas they would not for a woman. But otherwise I think they really experience all the same problems about this.

The men in our group are more active than the women, and they are coping very well. I really do think, though, that it is harder for a woman; I don't think it is so hard for a man. It is expected of you to do a job of work and come home and clean your house, do everything, whereas it is not for a man.

To conclude - how do you see the group developing, now that you have a regular committee?

Well apart from our local activities, eventually we have to have a representative on the London Region committee, which is different from the national level, and we will have to take part in these activities too.

I hope eventually that we do become more involved, personally - I do not know the views of all the other members, but certainly I would like to become far more involved, as I am far more interested in that side of Gingerbread.

10 Community action, women's aid and the women's liberation movement

Jalna Hanmer

To the extent that community action focuses on the issue of making a home rather than making a living, it would seem to be the province of women par excellence. (1) Yet their interests and visibility within community action struggles are often subliminal. One aim of this chapter is to speculate on why this happens and to suggest that women's aid by raising the fundamental nature of women's oppression within the family offers an important challenge to the view that to organise men in the community is adequately to represent the needs and interests of women. The dominance of men's interests and interpretations of social reality creates strategic and tactical problems for those who wish to fight women's exploitation and oppression within the community. I argue that this can happen only if issues are clearly defined as women's issues - as radical - and as community issues. Women's aid fits all three criteria.

The article begins by looking at the invisibility of women in community action and moves on to describe a community action organisation dominated by women and their interests, the National Women's Aid Federation (NWAF). (2) It is suggested that women's aid may not suffer the fate of other actions around women's interests because it tackles the central structure through which their oppression is organised - the family - and it is fed, osmotically so to speak, by the women's movement. By focusing on the family, women's aid exposes the difference between male and female roles, power and position in society. Differing values and conceptions about the family underwrite perceptions of male violence against women and how help should be offered, if at all. The article links apparently disparate analyses of the family and contrasts the similarity of the resulting practice with the very different action taken by the NWAF which provides refuges for women and is campaigning for changes in the law and law enforcement, housing policies and social security arrangements.

I do not discuss the history of violence against women within the family or the organisation and activities of refuges because these aspects are discussed by Angela Weir in chapter 11. The relationship between the women's movement and the NWAF is also discussed by Weir, but from a different perspective - that is that the women's movement

is only the spark that rekindled concern about wife-beating. She
argues that the crucial alliance for women's aid lies with community (i.e. local mixed and male) organisations, whereas this chapter comes to rather different conclusions. Where there is overlap
between the two chapters, therefore, this is specifically
because each is offering an alternative viewpoint, representing the
range of interpretations both within women's aid and more widely
within the women's movement.

COOLING OUT WOMEN

Community action involves a conjuncture between social movements
and organisations. Social movements last longer than mobs, masses,
crowds, yet they are not organisations. Social movements have a
group consciousness, a sense of belonging, an involvement in concerted action, yet technically one cannot join a social movement in
the sense that one joins an organisation. For example, to belong
or to be a member of the women's movement is a statement of psychological identification, not that of a card-carrying paid-up member
of X organisation.
    Social movements may have a mixture of formal organisations and
informal diffuse behaviour, or what Joe Banks describes as directed
and non-directed segments. (3) Directed have a formal leadership
structure, definitive ideology, stated objectives and specific
programmes, while non-directed involves a reshaping of perspectives
and values which occur through interaction. Community action is
involved in both processes, in particular creating directed segments
(or organisations) out of the non-directed. Stated like this, the
women's movement and its activities, including women's aid, should
be a clearly recognised part of community action, but community
action involves both an ideology and a practice that excludes women.
    The potential for serious change contained in community action
issues that highlight the differences between male and female roles,
power and position in society is rarely recognised. Campaigns in
which women are visible confirm their primary definition, for
example as child-minders. Thus in community action for child care
facilities, day care, playgroups, playgrounds, everyone is aware
that children and women may benefit from the provision, and the presence of women as organisers is not disputed. What is under question, however, is the radical nature of the demand. Child care is
not seen as radical or particularly political except to part of the
women's movement. Alternatively, when the activity is generally
agreed to be radical and based in large measure on local campaigning
and local groups, for example abortion and a woman's right to choose,
it may not be seen as community action as it is 'too political'.
    The ideological definition of women as irrelevant to social
change is pervasive, spanning from left to right political tendencies. (4) A recent unusually crude, and therefore particularly
revealing, exposition is to be found in 'Towards a New Social Work',
where J.R. Cypher argues: 'The drive, assertion and commitment
necessary for direct action are not generally features of women',
and that changes in sex roles do not necessarily affect female
sexuality which give rise to personal qualities that make commitment

to reform and the use of militant or conflict-laden approaches appropriate only for those with masculine personality traits. (5) According to this perspective, radical women are men in drag, and is a good example of a double-bind situation.

What is so interesting about linking a professional group (social work), radical action and sex is not merely the biologism of the argument but that it operates always in one direction. For instance, no one would dream of arguing that the reason why the social security system is not radical is because it is staffed largely by men. Also, to characterise social work as reactionary because it has so many women workers is to ignore that most senior positions are occupied by men even though they form a small proportion of the total work force. The argument ignores the issue of power.

A much more interesting and, I would argue, valid question arises from recognising that most social workers at the grass roots are women, as are most of their clients. (6) If the function of social work is largely that of social control, to put the usual 'left' argument crudely, who benefits from women controlling other women? That it is not women was obliquely recognised by radical social workers; witness the cover drawing in the 'Case Con' issue about women which showed a tower block filled with 'Why can't I cope' female clients with a female social worker sitting in her local office saying 'Why can't I cope?' (7)

Of course one could ask, is this saying anything more than that society and most of society's actors are widely believed both by men and women to be male? If we look at community work in relation to women, for instance, as with community action, both community workers and their participants are usually believed to be male. This is particularly interesting as the modern phase of community work (of which community action is a variant) dates from the late 1950s in Britain. Women were in a dominant position, but by the 1970s the Association of Community Workers, the main organisation of community workers, is largely male in membership and it seems to be generally agreed that community work is a man's activity. (8)

On the level of practice, the definition of women and their interests as irrelevant spans from spontaneous small group inter-action, for example what he says to she in a local tenants' associa-tion meeting, to concerted well-organised action, for example the attempt of one 'left' group to switch the emphasis of claimants' unions from unsupported mothers to unemployed men. (9)

On the small scale, women can be eliminated from decision-making and leadership by a variety of stratagems and what we need is a detailed analysis of these tactics in order to politicise women and improve their tactical skill. Examples from personal recent experi-ence with a middle-class residents' association range from the most crude, for instance not counting the women's votes in meetings, to the more subtle, for instance making sure that subcommittees have chairmen, by the male elite within the tenants' committee finding a man interested in the post and then turning around to the others (i.e. women and any males with the same low status) with a 'do you agree that Mr X (eminently well qualified, of course) should take the chair?' Subjected to this kind of treatment, women begin to exclude themselves - for instance at the tenants' committee meeting where the women, or some of them, sit one foot further from the edge of the table than the men, or fill the only roles genuinely open to them, the subservient tea-making and typing so well documented by the women's liberation movement. (10)

Further, women exclude themselves by not even attempting to work in these more formal organisations. In exploring networks of influence in a community, there is always the informal containing Mrs X who knows everyone and is helpful to everyone while occuping no formal leadership position of any kind whatever within the community. Thus the male power elite, through the formal political and welfare structures and community action organisations within the community, is shadowed by a female informal network of mutual aid. Sometimes this network erupts into a community campaign; more often it remains a reciprocal one arising out of and responding to both material and social poverty.

One of the factors that obscures a clear perception of community issues as women's issues is the place of women within the labour market. Much community action is up against organisations whose lower echelons are staffed by women; for example, the primary school, social work teams, housing departments (social security is an exception), so that at the grass roots community action participants face women across the counter. That these community structures are controlled by men is forgotten (and may seem irrelevant) as the struggle with the 'enemy' women proceeds.

Another is that every male organisation contains co-opted women who may have pulled up the trapdoor behind them, thereby excluding other women from getting in, and/or who act as the mouthpiece if male domination begins to be exposed. One frequent solution to an attack on male leadership in all types of organisations is quite unconsciously to field a woman to defend the organisational line and tactics when the going begins to get rough. (11) This tactic is almost invariably successful and has the effect of eliminating the threat that sexual politics be recognised as politics.

Concerted well-organised activity that furthers the interests of men at the expense of those of women may not be recognised as such. For example, prior to the direct action taken against the King Hill Hostel in 1965-6, Part III accommodation for the homeless was effectively limited to women and their children. While not all women were pleased to be in housing that their husbands could not enter, many were; unlike today, Part III was secure accommodation for battered women. The researchers on homelessness were well aware that one of its major causes was women leaving their husbands, often because of violence. (12) It was during the 1960s that concern with homelessness escalated, but it was not seen as politic to raise this issue, instead, the homeless needed to be sanitised and presented as ideal families with male hands who, through no fault of their own, had nowhere to live, which of course was true of many, especially in the metropolitan areas.

Some staff of Part III accommodation looked on the King Hill Hostel action with horror. They knew that the last thing many women in their care wanted was for their husbands to be admitted. Like the Greve Reports, this piece of community action was aimed at meeting the need of the dominant group, i.e. those who fitted society's stereotype of the ideal, at the expense of the worst off, i.e. those

who did not. The men who mounted the action at King Hill quite
naturally and unconsciously represented the interests of their own
group. (13)

As a result of the government decision in 1966 to open Part III
accommodation to husbands, battered women lost their refuges and
remained largely without until women's aid began. The effort to
provide refuges is still in its infancy, and all that is known about
need is that every time a refuge opens it is almost immediately full
to overflowing. (14) But what is new is that it is now politic to
campaign for battered women. The major intervening variable since
the time of the Greve Report and the King Hill action has been the
rise of the women's liberation movement.

WOMEN'S AID AND THE WOMEN'S LIBERATION MOVEMENT

The women's liberation movement has many strands and competing views
about the nature of the problems facing women and what is to be done
about them. Through participation in movement activities, whether
in consciousness-raising or definite campaigns, perspectives and
values can be transformed. Many women who have been touched by
this process, both lightly and profoundly, have become active in
women's aid. Their ability to empathise with battered women is born
of an understanding of their own oppression and exploitation.

There is a range of views within women's aid: the activists
share a sense of injustice, a knowledge that things are not as they
should be. Their emotional response ranges from compassion, sympathy and love for women to anger at the injustices committed
against them. The relationship of women's aid with the women's
liberation movement is real, if often elliptical and shadowy
rather than direct.

The majority of women's aid groups providing refuges in England
and Wales at the present time belong to the National Women's Aid
Federation. Women's aid began as a local activity with the opening
of a women's centre in Chiswick in 1971. By the beginning of 1974
there were over twenty local groups throughout Britain. The NWAF
was formed in March 1975 by thirty-five groups either planning or
running refuges for battered women. (15) Six months later the number
of member groups was over fifty with thirty-five houses between them,
and by March 1976 there were sixty-four groups with forty-six
refuges. (16) They came together to form a communication and support
network and to promote their interests at the national level. Groups
in Scotland were active in forming NWAF but, for purposes of funding,
set up a separate organisation, Scottish Women's Aid Federation,
later in 1975. While not formally linked, members from both national
organisations attend each other's conferences and collaborate infor-
mally in a variety of ways.

NWAF is organised around the autonomy of local groups. Individuals who wish to take part in its activities and various committees
must be active in a local group. (17) Decision-making power is
vested in the National Conference, which consists of all groups and
meets at least twice yearly. It has nine regions, which hold regular meetings where local and national issues are discussed. An
elected representative from each region attends the National

Co-ordinating Group, which meets every three months, where regional views are expressed on national issues.   NWAF maintains an
office in London and has several paid workers who are responsible
for co-ordinating the activities of the Federation. For charitable purposes NWAF is in the process of being registered as a
limited company, a legal form that fits its devolved organisation
more closely than would the traditional charity with trustees.

Collectively, NWAF provides a national open door policy. If a
woman contacts a refuge and the women there feel they are unable
to accept her because the refuge is already overcrowded, they will
contact another and usually in their region. (18) Because of the
problems inherent in moving, rehousing and schooling, groups try to
ensure that women are as close to their previous homes as they
wish to be.

The size and type of refuges vary. Some have as many as four to
five houses. Some have second-stage housing for women and their
children who must remain in a refuge for months while waiting for a
divorce or rehousing. A few have third-stage permanent housing,
sometimes with shared facilities - an option that many women would
like. Few groups are in a position to choose the size or type of
refuge they would like. To acquire any house at all is often a
major struggle. For example, the group in Nottingham have been campaigning for nearly two years for a house while the Leicester local
authority, before offering a house, demanded 100 local cases of
battering as proof that violence against women in marriage existed
as a serious problem. Where no co-operation is forthcoming, groups
may be forced to squat. Local authorities vary regionally in their
responsiveness; for instance on average it is much easier to gain
support in the Greater London area that in the north of England.

A few groups receive Urban Aid grants and a few have local
authority grants with amounts varying from several hundred to
several thousand pounds. Refuges with larger grants have paid non-
resident workers and play leaders, while groups without this rely
entirely on voluntary effort. Many groups are desperately poor,
surviving on jumble sales, donations and the rent allowance paid to
the women by social security, a sum which varies considerably from
place to place.

The forms of organisation utilised by women's aid have been
adopted from the women's movement, in particular the emphasis on
non-hierarchical democratic functioning. It is in daily life,
working through these forms of social organisation, that conflicts
will be dealt with, successfully or otherwise. The energy to try
to develop an alliance with one's worst-off sisters, rather than
settling for the traditional charitable relationship of helped and
helper, comes from the women's liberation movement. (19)

The ideal, a refuge managed largely by the women themselves with
the support group being just that - a support - is difficult to
achieve. While there are exceptions, usually women who come to
refuges are from the working class, while the support committees
that have set up and maintain the houses are composed of women from
the middle class. While in principle (i.e. women's liberation movement principle) women of all classes have more in common with each
other than with men (for in relation to the male within the family
and in society they share an inferior position), in practice it is

often difficult for these women to work closely with each other.
Not only have most of the support group women never been beaten as
have those living in the refuge, but also in the eyes of the women
who live there they have succeeded in meeting the problems of
acquiring an income, housing, and relationships with men.   Further,
the support group will inevitably find it difficult fully to share
decision-making and may consider themselves more able.   These and
no doubt other factors can create distance between the two.

A further gap between theory and practice is clearly visible at
NWAF committees and conferences, where the activists are largely
support committee members.

At present women's aid is radical action; like claimants' unions
and squatting, beleaguered by local authorities and relevant departments of national government, a directed segment that has arisen
out of the women's liberation movement.   This position, however,
could change, particularly if the movement loses its vitality.
Then assuming women's aid becomes sufficiently well supported by
state grants to fulfil a welfare function more cheaply than one
provided directly by the local authority, it could be transformed
into a traditional 'do-gooding' welfare activity, a completely
encapsulated organisation. (20)

Women's aid is clearly a women's issue.   The women's movement
with its questioning of accepted values and behaviour in male/
female relations ensures that a discussion of possible social
functions served by physical maltreatment of women within marital
relationships has a place on the agenda. (21)   And, to be practical,
only the collapse of the movement is likely to dislodge it.   Thus
the women's liberation movement can be described as a life insurance policy for women's aid.

Women's aid is a community issue in two ways: refuges are
locally based and supported and the family is widely believed to be
the basic unit of the community, the foundation of society.

LINKING THEORY AND PRACTICE: THE CENTRALITY OF THE FAMILY

Beliefs about the family affect views on the causation of marital
violence which, in turn, affect decisions on what ameliorative
action should be taken.   Explanations are crucial in determining
both the perception of the victim and her assailant and the response
of agencies.

The accepted paradigm of the family within academic sociology,
social work and the world at large is a functionalist one.   As Talcott
Parsons and Robert Bales explain, the primary functions of the
family are to regulate reproduction and to maintain the stability of
adult personalities. (22)   Or in the words of more popular writings,
it is a haven of warmth and caring in a competitive and cold world.
An analysis of the family in terms of power is not unheard of within
academic sociology merely rare.   In a recent article, W. Goode, for
example, argues that the family, like all social units, is a power
system resting to some degree on force or its threat. (23)   He describes force and its threat as one of four major sets of resources
by which people can move others to serve their ends.   The other
three are the economic, prestige or respect, and friendship or love.

As he points out: 'within the family itself, the harsh fact must
be faced that the member with the greater strength and willingness
to use it commands more force than others do. This is usually the
father'. (24) And by force, Goode means power. Also, in the
family, men usually have greater economic power, and greater prestige or respect accruing from being male and having more of the
first two sets of resources. Only in the fourth, friendship or
love, has the woman of the family a chance to equal or better the
resources held by the male.

While women's aid groups have no agreed position, the family as
a power system seems to be an implicitedly held model. A major aim
of the NWAF is 'To educate and inform the public, the media, the
police, the courts, the social services and other authorities with
respect to the battering of women, mindful of the fact that this is
the result of the general position of women in society'. (25) Their
role within the family is one expression of their inferior position in society, and as social inferiors it is to be expected that
many women will be physically assaulted by men at one time or
another, and some quite severaly and repeatedly.

Women's aid is not alone in advancing the idea that status varia-
tion is a cause of marital violence; so do the establishment within
the family sociology, where it is phrased rather differently. In
this model it is believed that general social change in the status
and roles of women is occurring, with women moving from a subordinate position to that of an equal partner in employment, family
duties and leisure activities. Different norms held by the husband
and wife about her behaviour, however, may lead to conflict, especially if the wife seeks to realise greater equality of status or if
the husband is uncertain of his superior status. This 'leads to a
need for men to re-emphasise. male dominance in the face of perceived uncertainty as to the legitimacy of such dominance'. (26)
Phrased like this, the focus is on the husband and his status problems rather than on the wife and hers.

While women's aid clearly may be seen as partisan, it is only
recently that the partisan position of academic sociology has begun
to be recognised. This coincides with the attack on functionalism,
the major system of thought within academic sociology. (27) While
neutral language may obscure the underlying value-judgments, within
functionalst theory stasis is the primary state and change a threat
to the social system. A balanced system is one in equilibrium, while
change is described as factors that create stress and disequilibrium.
In the above explanation it is the wife who is threatening the
system while the husband represents the status quo.

Others hypothesise a sub-culture of violence. (28) Some social
groups (in the past this was widely assumed to be the working class)
are believed to have more violent patterns of family interaction.
Sub-cultural behaviour is learned through socialisation by observing
parental interaction and through interaction with parents. In this
way the next generation of both sexes acquires the habit of beating
and being beaten.

Family socialisation is the currently popular explanation that
underwites the concept of the cycle of deprivation. This locates
the problem, if not in a particular identifiable group, at least
within individual families. Society as a whole remains untouched;

deviant behaviour is contained within those few carriers who, it is
hoped, only need identification and special treatment for them to
be restored to the community as 'healthy' functioning groups.

And then there are a variety of social-psychological and psychological explanations which are very much in vogue in the marital
guidance and social work fields. Explanations that focus on the personal psychological make-up may speak of the woman's 'need' to be
assaulted, or see the marriage relationship as working out the
great themes of love/hate and dominance/submission or arising when
an 'idealised partner fails' or as a result of a projection of
undesirable aspects of the self onto the other. (29)   Thus violence
may well arise and, indeed, can only be described as 'normal' behaviour. That this violence should almost invariably be from the male
to the female either is not seen as significant or is explained
biologically as arising from a man's or woman's 'nature'.

Direct evidence from women, and professionals who may be
involved with them, tends to reduce the problem to one of interaction between the couple or to the physical and psychological problems of one of them, thus creating a rag-bag of explanations,
partly factual, partly ideological. Brain damage, epilepsy and
toxic states are noted in some instances. Alcoholism and mental
illness is thought to be either a cause or a result of violent
marriage. The youth of the couples, a tendency for some women to
move from one violent relationship to another, violent reactions by
husbands to the pregnancy of their wives are observed and thought
to be caused by immaturity and the interaction of the personalities
of the couple and their expectations for each other. There are also
links between marital violence and non-accidental injury to children.

The DHSS see the problem as a lack of knowledge about the mecha-
nism of marital violence and the effects of different patterns of
intervention which creates a lack of confidence in professionals in
their approach to women or couples who may seek help. (30)   Thus
more research is needed for what is seen as a multifaceted problem,
to ensure skilled assessment of families and to know if children are
at risk of non-accidental injury so that action can be taken.

In practice, when the cause of violence in marriage is believed
to arise from the status or other problems of the husband, or from
psychological factors, the focus of the resulting action usually is
the woman, while the activity is euphuistically termed 'working with
families'. To work with the woman is to accept the power relations
within the family, possibly attempting to smooth off the too obvious
rough edges by sometimes successful attempts to see the husband,
while the woman is shored up with tranquillisers and social work
sessions. To be just, however, social workers have believed, and in
many areas no doubt rightly continue to do so, that women have no
options. Where refuges exist they are almost always used by social
workers and others to help women to change their lives.

When the problem is seen as arising from interaction or individual pathology, public policy issues may be discussed in terms of
the need for more social workers, more liaison between agencies
involved, broadening the functions of existing agencies (e.g. the
police should develop a welfare function), new forms of organisation such as family courts, the need to improve material provision
for the worst off, as more and better housing and financial support

is seen as a way to strengthen the family. (31) At root, these explanations take a functionalist view of the world, devaluing the problems of the woman in their efforts to regain equilibrium with a minimum of change.

Women's aid, with an analysis of the family that sees the woman as occupying an inferior position, focuses on gaining protection for her and her children, first through the provision of refuges and secondly, by changes in public policy in the key areas of police activity, the law, housing policies and financial support. First, a place of safety is found for her and then the battle begins to make the community a safe place for her. This is interpreted by others as a pro-woman stance.

If a woman decides to return to her husband, nothing could be easier, but if she decides to start a new life elsewhere, nothing could be more difficult. To do this she needs an income, somewhere to live for herself and almost always her children, and often con-tinuing protection from her husband or cohabitee from whom she may have every reason to fear renewed attack, should he find her. To date, the dominant campaign tactic of women's aid has been that likely to be adopted by any powerless group in society, the use of shame. By shaming one's powerful opponents one can induce them to grant concessions. This is the meaning behind the endless case-histories of horrific violence perpetrated over the last twenty years, the use of the middle-class woman's case history, mixed with occasional sharp uncompromising attacks on all the established agencies and departments of local and national government from whom the battered woman needs help. So far, the skilful use of the media that is necessary for this tactic to succeed has worked. (32)

It played a major part in the decision to set up the House of Commons Select Committee on Violence in Marriage in 1975. This act gave the newly formed NWAF a pressing reason to reach some agreement quickly on policy issues and to adopt the tactic of providing expert evidence. It offered an opportunity to the NWAF to campaign for social policy changes. The evidence of the NWAF to the Select Committee was based on the difficulties many women had in attempting to determine their own futures. The Select Committee visited refuges in England and Scotland, and the NWAF, through its co-ordinator, Jo Sutton, following the developing scenario closely.

The hearings offered the first opportunity for opposing points of view to meet face to face, and demands for changes in law, policy and behaviour were followed up in sessions with the relevant govern-ment departments and others. Pointed questions were asked, some answers given, and an occasional change of practice in government departments occurred as the hearings proceeded. The proceedings of the Select Committee are a goldmine of attitudes, values and prac-tices; the most extensive research ever undertaken into how the com-munity see and treat battered women.

Enforcing the law

Of the five agencies most likely to be concerned with battered women - the police, medical services, social services, housing departments and social security - the police are the most likely to

be informed first. (33)   Not only have they the task of enforcing
the laws of the land but they are virtually the only agency that
offers a 24-hour service well known to the general public.   While
individual policemen vary in their response, on the whole there is
a lack of reaction to domestic disputes.   The police are not responsible for serving or enforcing non-molestation injunctions -
often the protection a woman must have to be able to live in the
community with a minimum of fear.   A barrister for the NWAF
referred to the existing system of issuing and enforcing injunctions as making the injunction 'not worth the paper it is printed
on'. (34)   This literally has the effect of forcing women and the
children into refuges where they may stay for many months awaiting
the sale of the house and division of the proceeds in the case of
home-owners, or until the local authority agrees to rehouse them
elsewhere, or until private rented accommodation is found.

Usually the police do not actively intervene to protect the wife,
and in their evidence to the Select Committee on Violence in
Marriage they explain why.   'Whilst it is accepted that a major
cause of crime is "the efficiency or otherwise of the police", it is
not accepted that this factor applies in the case of "battered
wives".   The main contributory cause of this syndrome is the
aggression factor and the psychological reasons for this are beyond
the scope of police to prevent.' (35)   While women's aid argues
that in incident after incident the police should have intervened,
but did not, the police themselves say: (36)

There is no need whatsoever for any change in the police role of
(1) enforcing the law or (2) dealing with husbands and wife
disputes.   That some husbands do assault their wives, even quite
seriously, and are not punished for it, is not the fault of the
police, but is caused by the 'human element reaction' in the
attitude of many such wives.   They are reluctant to take their
husbands to Court.

The Metropolitan Police memorandum to the Select Committee then goes
on to explain why, giving reasons women's aid also would agree with,
'they may fear reprisals, the family unit could be broken; and financial hardship could result should he be sent to prison.' (37)
However, the police assume that the woman should prosecute, never
themselves, and it is her fault if the law is not enforced.   The
police evidence thus concludes: 'No changes in legislation or
police practice could have any appreciable effect on the human
relationships in marriage involved.' (38)

This view seems to be related to a belief that the marital
relationship should not be broken and a more active intervention on
their part on behalf of the wife might lead to this result.   Thus the
Association of Chief Police Officers of England and Wales and Northern Ireland in their evidence to the Select Committee say: (39)

Whilst such problems take up considerable Police time during say,
12 months, in the majority of cases the role of the Police is a
negative one.   We are, after all, dealing with persons 'bound in
marriage', and it is important, for a host of reasons, to maintain the unity of the spouses.   Precipitated action by the Police
could aggravate the position to such an extent as to create a
worse situation than the one they were summoned to deal with.   The
'lesser of two evils' principle is often a good guideline in these
situations.

The police seem to be taking on the task of concilation which is consistent with their attitude towards refuges for battered women. The memorandum accepts the need for temporary shelter, but goes on to say: 'Every effort *should be made to re-unite the family*' (emphasis theirs). (40)

What is under dispute is whether or not the rights of individuals are of paramount importance with adequate protection to be given to each and every individual against violence or the threat of violence. In their evidence the police admit that they are more apt to act if the suspected victim is a child or if the assault takes place outside the home. While this may appear to be a simple case of concern for the institution of marriage overriding the legal rights of one of the marriage partners, outright hostility towards assaulted women occasionally shines through; 'it is submitted that the equal status of women in society today precludes any preferential treatment for them: otherwise the law could fall into disrepute.' (41)

In their running battle with the police, NWAF provided expert evidence to Jo Richardson, MP, who introduced a Private Member's Bill that will require police to assume responsibility for enforcing injunctions if passed. If this Bill becomes law, of necessity current practices will be modified. Given their attitudes, the struggle to modify police practices is likely to demand a prolonged campaign by NWAF and others who support battered women.

Housing

There is a direct relationship between the police, court action and housing. As one witness to the Select Committee explained, a woman knows that even if her husband appears in court charged with assault, 'he is the tenant of the house and he is going to return to that house.' (42) And a Select Committee member says: 'When we have asked women: "Why did you stay and put up with it?", they usually say: "Where could I go?" ' (43)

The position regarding rehousing is difficult and complex, and no quick overview can do more than mention some of the main issues. In the experience of women's aid groups, the worst situation is presented by those local authorities who do not accept that battered women are homeless until the divorce is final, which may take over a year. Their view is that she has a home to go to whenever she wants. The reason for this attitude seems to be that one of the main sources of increased housing demands arises from wives leaving their husbands. This has led the DHSS to view the problem of battered women as one of homelessness, as they see her first need to be for accommodation. (44)

One of the major demands made by NWAF was that battered women be recognised as homeless, and in their evidence to the Select Committee the DHSS declared that local authorities do have a statutory obligation to provide temporary accommodation for battered wives as their need is urgent and unforeseeable. (45) The London Boroughs Association in their report on battered women have called on all their members to accept this interpretation and it may be that housing authorities will agree to change their policy without new legislation. (46)

Even if this is so, however, it is only a small step in the direction of rehousing battered women and their children. If a woman has been living in a council flat, the tenancy is almost always in her husband's name; and even if in their joint names it is only when the divorce is final and the woman awarded custody of the children that many local authorities will consider transferring the tenancy to the woman, and then only if there are no rent arrears. She may be held responsible for rent arrears even though she had not been able to occupy the home, and, of course, was given only one sum for the payment of rent by the Supplementary Benefits Commission who intended it for the home she was actually occupying, i.e. a place in the refuge. Further, even if the local authority finally agrees to transfer the tenancy the woman may need to live elsewhere in the city if her husband is likely to attack her again, but the local authority may not be prepared to offer her another place. If a woman comes from another area, which is likely as battered women often feel safer the further away they are from their husbands or cohabitees, the chance of rehousing is further reduced. Particularly in urban areas the supply of cheap, private rented property (the only remaining option for these poorest of women) is dwindling, while demand rises.

As a result of these problems NWAF makes a number of detailed recommendations to the Select Committee, to make it easier for women to be rehoused within and between housing authority areas, and to oblige local authorities to transfer tenancies to battered women who should not be held responsible for rent arrears run up by their husbands or cohabitees. (47) Also, in addition to providing housing to voluntary groups for refuges, NWAF recommends that local authorities make other accommodation temporarily available for women who no longer need emergency provision but need to be somewhere safe while waiting for divorce and possible property settlements to be completed. This happens in a few local authorities, and is far more satisfactory for the women and her children, as the constantly changing membership of the refuge, with its cramped quarters (two families often share one room), is not an ideal environment when a stay of some months is inevitable. While no one knows the potential extent of the demand, problems with rehousing is a major reason for refuges to become overcrowded. Much as the women in them would like to become permanently settled elsewhere, they cannot leave until housing is found for them.

The unequal position of women in society is summed up by the Chairman of the Select Committee, who asks, 'why should it be the wife and children who have to leave and not the husband? ... Why should we not create hostels to receive the battering husbands?' (48) Once again law enforcement and housing interlock. Without adequate police and court protection, a woman cannot stay in her own home even if the husband were removed, and to send the battering husband to a hostel presupposes the legal power and will to do so. Why should the husband voluntarily take himself to a hostel when he has the power of greater physical force and what amounts to the support of the state in its use? To suggest that the man should leave rather than the woman is to turn everything upside down, for in relation to the man the wife is his dependent, both legally and financially, as are any children they may have. (49)

An adequate income

The third area of greatest need for a woman who has left her husband or cohabitee is for an adequate income, and almost all women
who come to refuges must look to the Supplementary Benefits Commission for financial support. Most women have children of whom
one or more are often under school age, and few of the women, as
is true of the female population as a whole, possess the skills or
training that enable them to take the kind of paid employment
that commands an income adequate to maintain themselves and the
domestic help they then need. The women who are in paid employment before coming to a refuge may have to give up work under the
stress of marital violence, a change of residence and the demands
of their children. However, most women who come to refuges are
not in paid work, since they were totally, rather than partially,
dependent upon their husbands financially. Supplementary Benefit
enables a woman to survive apart from her husband or cohabitee,
but one-parent families are among the poorest in Britain, and none
more so than those dependent on the Supplementary Benefits
Commission.

   In its evidence, NWAF recommends implementing the Finer Committee
recommendations for a guaranteed maintenance allowance, but claim-
able within a month of separation; the introduction of the child
tax credit scheme, and also administrative orders which would
shift the responsibility for collective maintenance payments from
divorced, separated and unmarried mothers to the Supplementary
Benefits Commission. It asked for changes in DHSS procedures to
make it more difficult for a husband to trace his wife - which was
agreed - and for grants to women to be increased with discretionary
and emergency payment to be more readily available, for rent payments on the women's previous home to be continued so that no
arrears occur, and for a sympathetic visiting officer to be assigned
to local refuges.

   In examining the evidence given to the Select Committee by the
DHSS and DOE, it is clear that these departments are more subtle
than the police in their dealings with others over the issues of
battered women and those organisations that represent them. (50)
But whether or not they are more positively oriented towards solving
their problems is an issue yet to be determined.

THE FUTURE: ROUND TWO

The interim report of the Select Committee contained a number of
recommendations, including the funding of NWAF, that should assist
the continued growth of women's aid and further its point of view on
a number of social policy issues. NWAF is now in receipt of a grant
from the DHSS for their national office and staff for 1975-6. The
problem officially exists; round one is over, with women's aid winning on points.

   We now should expect the focus of interest to shift to its etio-
logy with an intensification of ideological warfare over the next
few years. Research will become a major weapon. The DHSS is currently funding a variety of as yet largely unnamed university

research projects to look at marital interaction and how the
immediate needs of the women who leave home because of violence
can best be met. The DOE is interested in research into housing
need and current practice in housing ex-battered women.

While basically atheoretical, strands within the women's liberation movement are struggling to tease theory out of the life
experience of women today, and battered women present a challenge
that cannot be ignored. Many must create new lives for themselves
and their children; thus potentially they become a vanguard, and
their problems in achieving a better life, the problems of all women.

The prize is considerable. Can the family, i.e. male-female
power relations, be kept more or less the same, or is change, i.e.
greater female freedom from male domination, going to take place?
For the powerless to succeed they need to gain allies such as the
press and influential others, and to remain united within their own
group. The present strategy of NWAF is to extend the network of
refuges and to campaign for social policy changes. To these must
be added a third major task, the need for NWAF to develop its own
analysis of violence against women within the family.

Women's aid offers an opportunity for women to become visible
as social actors involved in radical struggle against a formidable enemy, male dominance. For the time being it seems that
more or less separately organised community action is the only way
forward for women who wish to fight women's exploitation and
oppression in the community; where they can explore ways of fighting and winning a better bargaining position through attempts to
help the worst off. This is necessary because the subsidiary position of women in society inevitably makes males per se and their
interpretation of the situation dominant in community action (as
elsewhere), even though the activity is around issues that involve
and affect both sexes.

Success will further an analysis of the patriarchy and may, if
not flesh out the bones of feminist theoretical writings that see
women as the class, or as a caste, further an analysis that will
gain yet more adherents among both men and women for a restruc-
turing of interpersonal relationships between them.

Notes

1 R. Frankenburg, 'Communities in Britian', Pelican, 1966, refers
   to community studies as the industrial sociology of the housewife.
2 I would like to thank the many women of NWAF with whom I have
   talked and worked. While this has shaped and aided the development of my views, I of course take full responsibility for the
   opinions expressed in this article.
3 'The Sociology of Social Movements', Macmillan, 1972.
4 For a refutation of this view see M.R. dalla Costa and S. James,
   'The Power of Women and the Subversion of the Community,
   Bristol, Falling Wall Press, 1972.
5 Social reform and the social work profession: what hope for a
   'rapprochement', in H. Jones, ed., 'Towards a New Social Work',
   Routledge & Kegan Paul, 1975, p.17.

6 Recognising that both worker and client are women is much more
   difficult than it would appear at first as the tortured use of
   personal pronouns in the literature testifies. Usually all
   social workers and their clients are male, or if by a fluke
   somehow a social worker is identified as female the client
   remains male, making one marvel at the effect of ideology on
   perception.
7 Spring 1974.
8 I am thinking of Muriel Smith and Ilys Booker's work with what
   is now known as the Association of London Housing Estates in the
   late 1950s and early 1960s, and Ilys Booker's next project in
   Notting Dale. Accounts of both have been published, G.
   Goetschius, 'Working with Community Groups', Routledge & Kegan
   Paul, 1969 and R. Mitton and E. Morrison, 'A Community Project
   in Notting Dale', Allen Lane, 1972.
9 H. Rose, Up Against the Welfare State, in R. Miliband and J.
   Saville, eds. 'The Socialist Register 1973', Merlin, 1974,
   pp.179-203.
10 For a stunning account see B. Jones and J. Brown, 'Towards a
   Female Liberation Movement', New England Free Press (originally
   published by Southern Student Organising Committee), 1968.
11 The ease and apparently non-collusive way in which this tactic
   is introduced makes one think of symbiosis.
12 Personal communication from Dr Muriel Brown. See for example
   the first Greve Report, J. Greve, 'London's Homeless',
   Occasional Papers in Social Administration 10, Bell, 1964;, M.
   Brown, 'Problems of Homelessness', MSCSS, 1964; B. Glastonbury,
   'Homeless near a Thousand Homes', Allen & Unwin, 1971.
13 See R. Bailey, 'The Squatters', Penguin, 1973, for an account of
   this campaign.
14 Report from the Select Committee on Violence in Marriage, vol.2,
   Report, Minutes of Evidence and Appendices, HMSO, 1975,
   recommends that there should be 1 place in a refuge for each
   10,000 population.
15 Erin Pizzey of Chiswick Women's Aid chose not join NWAF and at
   root her refusal is an issue about power and control.
16 There are member groups in Acton, Bath, Bexley, Brighton,
   Bristol, Bury St Edmunds, Camden, Doncaster, Exeter, Greenwich,
   Great Yarmouth, Hackney, Hammersmith, Haringey, Hassocks,
   Havering, Hastings, Hemel Hempstead, Hove and Portslade, Hudders-
   field, Hull, Islington, Lambeth, Leeds, Leicester, Lewisham,
   Luton, two in Manchester (Manchester and Manchester Shield),
   Milton Keynes, Newcastle on Tyne, Nottingham, Norwich, Oxford,
   Reading, St Albans, Sheffield, Southend, Southampton, Southwark,
   Stevenage and North Herts, Sunderland, Sutton, Swindon, Tower
   Hamlets, Wandsworth, West Sussex, West Cumbria, Waltham
   Forest and Redbridge, York, Cardiff, Bromley, Dorset, Enfield,
   Kensington, Newham, North Tyneside, Nuneaton, Salford, Stockport,
   Wellingborough and Westminster. The groups in Scotland are in
   Aberdeen, Drumchapel, Dundee, Edinburgh, Glasgow, Falkirk and
   Stirling.
17 The practial meaning of this basic principle has begun to be
   tested. In one refuge, a support committee member has been
   defined as one who is known to the women living in the house.

18   Battered women are not accepted only from member groups but
     also from others, such as Chiswick Women's Aid, who for inst-
     ance on occasion puts women into taxis and without warning
     sends them to other London refuges.
19   The concept of worst off implies a continuum of violence from
     none to murder and is based on knowledge that all women have of
     male violence and its threat. This knowledge is acquired
     through direct personal experience of violence from fathers
     or brothers or boyfriends or husbands and by hearsay from
     friends, acquaintances and others of whom they have heard.
     Many women recognise that there is an element of luck in not
     being at the far end of the continuum, i.e. among the worst off.
20   H. Rose and J. Hanmer, Community participation and social
     change, in D. Jones and M. Mayo, eds, 'Community Work Two',
     Routledge & Kegan Paul, 1975, for a discussion of the distinc-
     tion between co-opting individuals and encapsulating organisa-
     tions.
21   See B. Warrior, Battered lives, 'Houseworkers' Handbook',
     Women's Centre, Cambridge, Mass., 1974, pp.25-46.
22   'Family, Socialisation and Interaction Process', Routledge &
     Kegan Paul, 1956.
23   Force and violence in the family, 'Journal of Marriage and the
     Family', 33 (4), 1971, pp.624-36.
24   ibid., p.628.
25   The other four aims and objects of NWAF are: 1. To provide
     temporary refuge for women who have suffered mental and physical
     cruelty and their children on request. 2. To encourage the
     women to determine their own futures and to help them achieve
     it, whether it involves returning home or starting a new life
     elsewhere. 3. To recognise and care for the emotional and
     educational needs of the children involved. 4. To offer
     support, advice and help to any woman who asks for it, whether
     or not she is a resident, and also to offer support and after-
     care to any women and children who have left the refuge.
26   N. Miller, 'Battered Spouses', Occasional Papers on Social
     Administration no. 57, Bell, 1975, p.14. This pamphlet gives a
     useful resume of theories of the causation of violence in
     marriage as do R. Dobash and R. Emerson Dobash, Violence between
     Men and Women within the Family Setting, paper presented at
     VIII World Congress of Sociology, Toronto, 1974.
27   For instance see A. Gouldner, 'The Coming Crisis of Western
     Sociology', Basic Books, New York, 1970.
28   M. Wolfgang and F. Ferracuti, 'The Sub-culture of Violence:
     Towards an Integrated Theory in Criminology', Tavistock, 1967.
29   H. Dicks, 'Marital Tension', Routledge & Kegan Paul, 1967; A.
     Storr, 'Human Aggression', Penguin, 1968.
30   Report ... on Violence in Marriage, p.99.
31   Miller, op. cit.
32   Erin Pizzey of Chiswick Women's Aid is particularly adept in
     utilising the technique of shame, see 'Scream Quietly or the
     Neighbours will Hear', Penguin, 1974, and also National Women's
     Aid Federation, 'Battered Women Need Refuges', NWAF, 1975.
33   When discussing social policy issues, this article describes
     aspects of the situation in England and Wales only. While in

many ways the experiences of battered women and refuges is
similar, Scotland has a different legal system.   A difference
of particular importance to battered women is that a second
witness is needed to corroborate assault.   In 1975 the
Scottish Home and Health Department proposed to fund Scottish
Women's Aid Federation.

34   Report ... on Violence in Marriage, p.81.
35   ibid., p.378.
36   ibid., p.377.
37   ibid.
38   ibid.
39   ibid., p.366.
40   ibid., p.369.
41   ibid., p.378.
42   ibid., p.281.
43   ibid.
44   ibid., pp.479, 481.
45   ibid., p.103.
46   ibid., Appendix 15, p.505.
47   ibid., pp.59-62.
48   ibid., p.190.
49   'The Demand for Independence', The Women's Liberation Campaign
     for Legal and Financial Independence, November 1975.
50   ibid., pp.98-118, 450-5, 176-9.

11 Battered women: some perspectives and problems

Angela Weir

Battered women have become the cause célèbre of English domestic life. So much so that the French Minister for Women's Affairs recently referred to wife-battering as an English malaise. (1) This statement is almost certainly untrue and probably indicates a confusion with the more traditional 'vice anglais', but it does demonstrate the wide publicity which has been given to the problem in the United Kingdom, culminating in the setting up of a Parliamentary Select Committee in February 1975 to examine and make recommendations on 'the problems of families where there is violence between the partners'. (2) The background to this publicity has been the setting up of refuges for battered women in England, Scotland, Wales and Ireland. The scale of the problem has been revealed in almost a geometrical progression as more refuges are set up.

The purposes of this article are to examine the causes of this sudden concern. Historically it is argued that the problems of battered women are visible only when there has existed a women's movement concerned with the specificity of women's oppression. However, differing understandings of the causes of this oppression have led to very differing solutions being posed. The concern of the nineteenth-century agitators with improving the material conditions of life and achieving legislative changes is contrasted with the present campaign to set up refuges for battered women. It is argued that the concept of a refuge owes much to the ideas of self-help and autonomous organisation elaborated by the Women's Liberation Movement, although the problems of battered women attract a sympathy and desire to help from a very broad section of women in society, and, perhaps ironically, working in or for a refuge is one way in which women come into contact with the ideas and practice of the WLM. The organisation and aims of the National Women's Aid Federation is discussed in more detail by Jalna Hanmer. She also suggests that it is necessary for the NWAF and local refuges to pursue a separatist strategy. That is to say that women must organise separately in the community to fight against their exploitation. She does not consider the problem of alliances with mixed groups, which this chapter attempts to deal with. (In describing this strategy as 'separatist', I do not wish to suggest that any

allusion is being made to lesbian life-style politics.) While
arguing that the problems of battering can be understood and
resolved only in the context of a feminist analysis of women's
oppression, I suggest that the result of such a separatist strategy
may well be to enforce the view that battered women are a 'special
problem' for whom 'special' provision is needed. In relation to
housing, for instance, it is argued that campaigns to make local
authorities accept an obligation to rehouse battered women will
involve fundamental changes in local authority housing policy.
By basing housing need on the unit of the nuclear family, all housing authorities grossly underestimate the amount of accommodation
needed. In campaigns to reverse this policy it is possible, and may
well be necessary, for Women's Aid to seek alliances with other
groups campaigning for more and improved housing provision, and to
raise these issues among more traditional working-class organisations in the tenants' and trade union movement. While it is
accepted that this will involve challenging male privilege and
assumptions of female dependence on men, it is argued that this
process is an important aspect of the work of Women's Aid, and
provides a forum in which to raise the ideological and material
oppression of women, both locally and nationally.

To gain some perspective on the issue, it is instructive to look
back just over a hundred years to the last occasion when the battered wife impinged on the public conscience. In 1851, for instance,
John Stuart Mill wrote an article in the 'Sunday Times' entitled,
'Protection of Women', which in its use of horrifying examples to
provoke public indignation might well have come straight from a
chapter of Erin Pizzey's book, 'Scream Quietly or the Neighbours
Will Hear', an account of her experiences at Chiswick Women's Aid.
(3) He cites examples of a bulldog set at the heels of a wife, blows
with the poker, attempted murder by hanging, stabbings, murder in a
fit of drunkenness. (4) His concern, like that of modern activists,
was with providing some effective means of escape for these women.
The lack of a legal remedy for the working-class wife also informed
an influential article by J.W. Kaye, 'Outrages on Women', published
in 1856. (5) However, Kaye's conceptualisation of the problem and
the reforms he proposed are very different from present-day discussion. Kaye attempted to explain the incidence of physical brutality to working-class women by suggesting that the appalling
material conditions of the working class, particularly the housing
conditions, transformed aggression (which would have manifested
itself in sophisticated mental torture in the middle-class husband)
to rains of blows and unrestrained physical violence from the
working-class husband. He also connected material deprivation with
the working-class wife's ignorance of the domestic arts; which
explained, if it did not justify, the brutality of a husband denied
'a comfortable arm chair, a singing tea kettle, a tidied room', (6)
things that were his due after a hard day's work. In short, wife-
battering was seen as a symptom of the brutalisation of working-
class life, albeit from a liberal, bourgeois point of view. (7)

The solution was posed in terms of alleviating the material
distress of the underprivileged classes, largely through philan-
thropic good works and female education in the domestic arts and in
providing some effective legal remedy for working-class women who

had been assaulted by their husbands. The efforts of nineteenth-
century philanthropists to improve and reform the working class have
been well documented elsewhere. (8) The measure which gave
working-class women legal redress was the Matrimonial Causes Act
1878 which conferred on magistrates courts the power to grant a
separation order with maintenance to a wife whose husband had been
convicted of aggravated assault on her. Frances Power Cobbe, who
campaigned for this reform, outlines her arguments in a pamphlet
called 'Wife Torture':

> After much reflection I came to the conclusion that in spite of
> all the authority in favour of flogging the delinquents, it was
> not expedient on the women's behalf that they should be so
> punished, since after they had undergone such chastisement,
> however well merited, the ruffians would inevitably return more
> brutalised and infuriated than ever; and again have their wives
> at their mercy. The only thing really effective, I considered
> was to give the wife the power of separating herself and her
> children from the tyrant. Of course, in the upper ranks, where
> people could afford to pay for a suit in the Divorce Court, the
> law had for some years opened to the assaulted wife the door of
> escape. But among the working class, where the assaults were
> ten-fold as numerous and twenty times more cruel, no legal means
> whatever existed of escaping from the husband returning after
> punishment to beat and torture his wife again.

While this reform probably provided relief for many women, it also
introduced a separate and secondary matrimonial procedure with different rules and administration especially for the cruder require-
ments of the poor. It is ironic that today, when the problems of
battered women have again come to light, the Law Commission is
endeavouring to deal with these anomalies and bring the ground for
obtaining separation orders in the magistrates courts in line with
those now operating in the divorce courts. (9)

THE LONG SILENCE: WOMEN'S NEW ROLE

It is difficult to explain why after the agitation of this period
the problem virtually disappeared for a hundred years. Clearly a
detailed historical analysis is much called for. Here it is possible to suggest only a number of factors which may have been significant. The real improvement in social and housing conditions,
shorter working hours and the increased earning power of working-
class men, the gradual exclusion of women as equals from the labour
market, the falling birthrate - all contributed to and made possible the elaboration of the woman's role as wife and mother. (10)
Substantial improvements in the material conditions of working-
class life and the changes in family structure, particularly the
role of the wife and mother, may, in fact, have reduced the overall
incidence of violence against wives and cohabitees. Kaye may have
been right about the comfortable arm chair and the singing kettle,
although it would require a historical examination of police statistics and other contemporary records to demonstrate this. However,
given the analysis of the earlier reformers, it was natural that
once the conditions of the poor did improve and more legislation

was passed to give formal rights to women, concern for the battered
woman was likely to abate. (11)

THE INFLUENCE OF THE WOMEN'S LIBERATION MOVEMENT

The feature common to the agitation of the later part of the nine-
teenth century and the twentieth century is the existence of a
women's movement. It is this which led people such as Mill and
Frances Power Cobbe to be especially concerned with the violence
experienced by the working-class woman and to champion her cause.
The difference now is that the apparent universality of the nuclear
family, the absence of clear and dramatic inequalities of wealth
and privilege, and the ideology of the cold war, have created a
situation where women are more likely spontaneously to recognise
the antagonisms between men and women, rather than perceiving
women's oppression in direct class terms.

The historical configuration out of which the contemporary
women's movement has grown has, I think, affected the understanding
of the problem of battered women in two general ways. First, the
recognition that women have a common oppression over and above, or
even prior to, class boundaries makes possible an emotional and
political identification between women in different classes and
situations which has previously been impossible. Practically, this
has meant that many women in a relatively privileged position have
been able to cut through some of the swathes of philanthropy so
strong in the middle-class tradition. This is not to say that this
ideological identification can always be articulated in reality.
There are many material and cultural factors which separate battered women from other women in society and from each other. The
experience of many refuges has been partially an acknowledgment and
coming to grips with these differences, particularly for working-
class women. However, the identification has provided, in refuges,
a mutual meeting-point and an important new space for development.

Second, although the ideological assumptions of the norm of happy
family life are very strong, where Philip and Katy salivating Oxo
gravy march down the corridors of domestic bliss to be encircled by
the strong arms of family insurance, this make-believe is suscep-
tible to gross and violent examples of family breakdown. Hence the
considerable public outcry over battered wives and children. Despite any previous conspiracy of silence that may have existed once
the phenomenon had been publicly demonstrated, it becomes necessary
to advance explanations and remedies to prevent more serious erosion
of the goals and ideals of British domestic life. (The crucial
importance of displaying stigmata to shame and exposure is, incidentally, illustrated by the fate of the Finer Report on one-parent
families. The publication of this Report, which must rank as one of
the most authoritative surveys of British family life, has coincided
with the agitation to do 'something' for battered women. Presumably
because one-parent families have fewer physical scars to display,
absolutely nothing is being done or intended to be done about Finer's
recommendations. (12))

THE DEVELOPMENT OF WOMEN'S AID CENTRES

Chiswick Women's Aid was founded almost accidently by a group of
women who took a house to start a 'Women's Centre' for local women
to drop in and discuss their problems. (13)   Although the publicity
that Erin Pizzey has created about the plight of battered women has
been extremely influential, it is difficult to explain the very
rapid public acknowledgment of the problems and the setting up of
new refuges except in terms of the sensitising influence of the
Women's Liberation Movement on public opinion and the infra-
structure of women's groups and individual women eager to help
their sisters.   Erin Pizzey was speaking to an audience already
softened up by Women's Liberation.

Two examples both quoted in the first pamphlet of the National
Women's Aid Federation, 'Battered Women need Refuges', (14) provide examples of the process.   The description of York Women's Aid
is as follows: (15)

To start with, all the women involved came from the Women's
Action Group connected with the university. As word got around
about our aims, other women joined us who had no previous
experience in the women's movement and the group now includes a
wide range of women, a solicitor, social workers and working
women from the town. Whatever our previous experience, most of
us have found that we have feminist ideas.

The York group go on to describe a successful meeting they held in
York to publicise the problems of battering and to emphasise the
need for a refuge there.   The meeting was attended by doctors,
(every doctor's surgery in York took a poster advertising the meeting), solicitors, social workers, local councillors and interested
members of the public.   Perhaps, though, the most interesting part
of the meeting was the initial decision to hold it in a 'posh
assembly hall', rather than the university where they could have had
a room free of charge.   They felt that if it was held at the university Tory councillors especially would be able 'to dismiss our
campaign as just another lot of student trouble-making'. (16)   By
avoiding this pitfall, they were able to unlock the politics of
women's liberation from the labelled politics of extremism and exert
maximum public pressure on a broad spectrum of powerful opinion.
The necessity for women's groups wishing to start a refuge to reach
out and convince 'straight' opinion has been an important two-way
process.   Many women have been able to gain insights and experience
of the power structure of their local areas, as well as organisational and negotiating skills, and on the other hand local authorities and statutory agencies have been confronted with a specific
example of the need for women's liberation backed by strong female
advocacy.   The York group say they felt confident in dealing with the
local authority, because 'We knew a lot more about the problems
facing battered women in York than most of the officials concerned
and we had the facts and figures to back up our case.' (17)

The process is not, of course, always as direct as this.   In the
same booklet, 'Battered Women Need Refuges', there is also an account
of the formation of a refuge in Manchester, 'Shield'.   This refuge
was started primarily by a group of social workers and probation
officers.   Their experience differs from that of other groups in

that as they were, so to speak, on the inside, they were able to
organise a smoother ride than some women's groups starting from
scratch with no knowledge or experience of local government.
However, although they point out that their approach to other
agencies has been based on consensus and co-operation, despite
private criticism they may have had, their group has in fact benefited from the public debate in the media, initiated by neighbouring Manchester Women's Aid, a group including many members of the
Women's Liberation Movement and influenced by its practice and
politics. They say: (18)

> The conflict inherent in any such debate was identified with
> Manchester Women's Aid and not with Shield. They certainly did
> a great deal to bring the plight of battered women to the notice
> of the public in Manchester and their actions in this area
> helped Shields to maintain a low profile which the local authori-
> ties appreciated. It is impossible to assess how much the con-
> flict helped Shields progress but it is probable that without
> Women's Aid Shield's case would not have been accepted and
> supported so energetically.

I do not wish to comment on the politics of this situation, but
merely point out the crucial role of feminist propaganda.

The effects of such propaganda has not, of course, been confined
to women actually identifying with the WLM. The issue of battered
women has also been taken up by a number of more traditional women's
organisations: Women's Sections of the Labour Party, Women's
Institutes, Townswomen's Guilds and Ladies' Circles. North Wales
Women's Aid, for instance, was pioneered by the Ladies' Circle in
Bangor, because 'women took an interest in the problem of women at
risk'. (19) In Scotland the Scottish Labour Women's Advisory
Committee chose the plight of battered women as their theme for
their activities in International Women's Year. In their evidence
to the Select Committee, they say: [We] deliberately chose this
issue for highlighting in International Women's Year because it
demonstrates both the degree of poverty and the extent of sex discrimination that still exists in our society today.' (20) Among
their other activities they had contacted every Labour group in the
old and new local authorities asking for information on what steps
had been taken to alleviate the problems of battered women. Last
year's TUC Women's Conference also called for immediate action to
help battered women. In moving the motion, Mrs Freda Good of the
Electricians' Union said: 'Cats and dogs are better treated than
some wives.' (21) The willingness of sections of the labour movement to take up the issue of battered women is in itself an example
of the increasing understanding and concern with the position of
women which has been largely prompted by Women's Liberation.

Resolutions calling for the government to provide short-stay help
for battered women also came from the annual conference of the
National Union of Townswomen's Guilds (22) and in June the National
Federation of Women's Institutes called on the government to take
immediate action to provide alternative accommodation for battered
wives. (23)

THE DOOR OF ESCAPE - THE CONCEPT OF A REFUGE

As indicated earlier, the idea of providing a refuge for battered
women arose almost accidentally out of the experience of a local
women's group in Chiswick starting up a women's centre and finding
that battered women came to them for help and refuge. The idea of
a Women's Centre did not, of course, arise accidentally. Women's
Centres grew out of the experience of the women's movement and a
number of such Centres have been set up around the country. So
on one level, at least, refuges for battered women came directly
from the practice of the women's movement. The concept of a refuge,
however, also involves other important principles of the women's
movement.

First, the demand for a refuge is very action orientated. It
involves an immediate time-scale where something can be done here
and now without waiting for long-term changes in legislation or
attitudes. As such, it underlines the idea that women can help
themselves and each other. A member of a support group writing in
the NWAF pamphlet expresses this position: (24)

Because of the unremitting pressure of the women's movement
women are beginning to take a closer look at the situation they
are in, and if it is a bad one, to take steps to change it.
Many are no longer prepared to play the little woman who sits
back and takes what's coming to her. Before refuges existed,
women were ashamed to talk about being beaten, and just accepted
the situation they were in.

Second, the concept of self-help, which has always been crucial
to the WLM, is, in fact, very applicable to the organisation of a
refuge. Women can not only elect to change their lives, but the
very process of election can increase a woman's independence.
Leeds Women's Aid make the point: 'In order to make the refuge
democratic and co-operative and to enable each woman who comes to
it to regain self respect and confidence, the refuge is run so
that every woman is able to contribute what she can to its functioning.' (25) The importance of self-help is also underlined in an
account by Norwich Women's Aid in the same pamphlet. They emphasise
the co-operation they have received from the local authority and end
on a slightly apologetic note: (26)

This description of the way we operate must sound very welfare
orientated and complacent to other groups facing bigger struggles
in difficult urban areas. But the co-operation we receive in no
way implies interference in the way Leeways is run. The day to
day running of the refuge and the last say in taking new referrals is left to the families. Volunteers do not go to the house
except at stated times, or by invitation. The families pay rent
and while they are with Leeways it is their home to be used as
they wish.

These may, of course, be read as idealised statements on intent
rather than factual descriptions of experience. Undoubtedly the
success of co-operative self-help depends on a number of variables:
the size of the house, and the facilities available - especially for
children - the ratio between staff and/or volunteers and women, the
average length of stay of the women and no doubt a number of other
factors. The problem of creating clear boundaries of behaviour which

are mutually chosen and acceptable must remain a constant political process rather than a matter of blueprint, but although all refuges have had to grapple with these problems, many refuges have achieved a successful level of operation based upon the principles of self-help. Members of the National Women's Aid Federation are at present discussing a forthcoming pamphlet which will examine these problems in more detail and also consider the relevance of this form of organisation in other residential situations.

LOCAL ACTIVITY

Posing the solution in terms of a refuge also means that there is considerable incentive for local activity. It was suggested earlier that in the nineteenth-century, the solution to the problem of battered women was posed at a long-term national level, legislative reform and the amelioration of working-class conditions. A refuge, by contrast, is a realisable goal, even in an era of social service cutbacks. One practical effect of the emphasis on self-help is that it considerably cheapens the cost of the operation. To get a refuge going, all that is needed is a house, and the cost is not necessarily inflated by the need to employ paid workers, residential staff or other expert services. Even a house can be obtained by squatting if no other means is forthcoming. In turn, the less costly the operation the less control the financing body is likely to demand and the more incentive there is for local groups to campaign with the prospect of not only getting a refuge, but also having considerable control over any resources they manage to win. The idea of providing help through a refuge acted as a spur to local activity and simultaneously spread concern about the situation of battered women at grass-roots level.

Here, however, the relationship of Women's Aid with more traditional forms of community work is unclear. At an immediate level the function of a refuge is to take a woman out of the community and provide protection from other members of the community - husbands, relatives, boyfriends - who may, through force or manipulation, be trying to get the woman back. The necessary secrecy which surrounds the location of a refuge emphasises this point. If community work is defined as mobilising human and material resources in a defined geographical neighbourhood to achieve a common end, then Women's Aid does not fit easily into this model.

A more radical, analytical model of community action is that which defines 'community' as those areas of life which take place away from the point of production, and community struggle as all those campaigns which are not recognisable as trade union activity. A specific version of this analysis, which has been elaborated by some tendencies within the Women's Liberation Movement, is that the basis of the community is the family, and women's oppressed position within the family. While this view has had a positive effect in providing a critical analysis of economistic political strategies and has again focused on the position of women in the family, in many respects the formulation is too vague theoretically to discern any clear strategies for action.

It has been argued previously that Women's Aid is a very practical

expression of the political analysis and practice of the Women's
Liberation Movement, and that, as such, it has considerable
political importance. However, to call this 'community action'
does not, of itself, indicate any analysis of the relationship
between Women's Aid and other sections of the community, including
local women's organisations, who may be campaigning for improvements in their conditions. It is possible to argue that there is
an inherent contradiction between men and women in society, but
this analysis rests on grounds other than the concept of the
community per se. If a separatist feminist analysis is introduced
to describe women organising in the community, then the logic of
this analysis is that the male/female conflict overrides all other
forms of working-class community organisations. Women become
another competing section of the community who share objective
interests with more traditional working-class organisations in the
community such as tenants' associations or trades councils, or even
with newer forms of community activity - free schools, law centres,
community action groups, etc.

While I disagree with the position that there is an absolute
contradiction between the interests of men and women in society,
it is nevertheless useful, here, to examine the consequences of
this view for Women's Aid in local communities. If women's
refuges are to shun all other local community interests, this could
easily end in our acquiescence in society's official definition of
battered women as yet another problem minority group - in this
case the 'inadequate' women who have not managed to get themselves
together. From here, the next step would be for them to be sub-
sumed under the general social services umbrella of similar organisations, voluntary or statutory, set up to deal with groups of
'inadequates' such as 'black youth' and the 'mentally disabled'.

The problems are very clearly illustrated by the struggles that
are already going on for recognition of battered women as homeless
and for rehousing them. What is required is a radical change in
local authority housing policy: what may well be offered as a
strategy to deal with the problem is the provision of a few special-
ised nominations to housing associations. For some housing associations to gather battered women under their aegis would no doubt
help in their empire-building efforts, but it would not alter the
policies of the local authorities, who must be the main providers of
housing. A few women would have been rehoused, some might even be
able to get joint tenancies, but basically the demands would have
been defused and no radical change achieved.

If Women's Aid is to campaign successfully for a radical change
in housing policy and practice it is natural, as well as necessary,
to seek alliances with other groups, tenants' organisations, campaigns for the homeless and single, one-parent family groups who are
also making similar demands. No alliance is ever an easy one, and in
this case Women's Aid will have to confront and challenge the male
chauvinism which exists in most working-class organisations.
However, this process in itself is one of the most crucial battles
for Women's Aid. We are campaigning not for pity or sympathy, but
for structural changes which would help eradicate battering.

From personal experience it is already possible to see this process occuring, albeit in an uneven way. A local federation of

tenants recently waged a campaign over a battered woman who was
being evicted by the council because of her husband's arrears. At
the same time, some of the male tenants clearly felt uneasy about
the personal questions involved in the relationship between men and
women that Women's Aid inevitably raises.

THE NATIONAL WOMEN'S AID FEDERATION

There was an early move to consolidate the various local groups and
create a National Federation of Women's Aid Groups. Whatever a
refuge's connection with other local groups, all refuges are thrown
into a direct relationship with various government departments,
particularly the Department of Health and Social Security, the
Department of the Environment, the Home Office and the Lord
Chancellor's Department. Some of these powers are delegated to
local authorities, but as local government is run on party political
lines, the need for a national organisation is again clear.

The National Women's Aid Federation was formed in March 1975 and
is probably the first national organisation whose perceptions and
practices are informed by the Women's Liberation Movement to receive
government finance. The Federation has so far sought to preserve
this allegiance by using forms of participatory democracy that have
been evolved by the women's movement. This structure has of itself
allowed people with differing views to work alongside each other
and to be involved in the organisation. However, increasingly vital
for the Federation's work is our understanding and articulation of
the causes of battering.

SETTING APART - A PATHOLOGICAL PROBLEM?

An examination of the causes of battering are not within the scope
of this paper, but it is already possible to distinguish two clear
positions, one which sees battering as a function of women's
generally oppressed position in society and the other which explains
battering in terms of the individual pathology of men who batter
and women who are battered. This latter view is clearly expressed
by Erin Pizzey, who says in her evidence to the Select Committee:
(27)

> In a democratic society laws are made for reasonable men. To
> legislate against violent husbands would penalise the majority
> of people who only need a reminder that the law exists to pro-
> tect us all against anti-social behaviour. These men are out-
> side the law; they have been imprinted with violence since child-
> hood so that violence is part of their normal behaviour ... I
> believe that many of the children born into violence grow up to
> be aggressive psychopaths, and it is the wives of such men that
> we see at Chiswick. I feel that the remedies lie in the hands
> of the medical profession and not in the court of law because the
> men act instinctively, not rationally.

Her view is supported, in essence, by Dr Gayford, who studied the
cases of 100 women staying at Chiswick, and apparently focused on
pathological features common to battered women such as short

courtships and early and unplanned pregnancies! (28) Given these
views, it is hardly surprising that the solutions and policies they
propose are primarily treatment-orientated, i.e. more refuges,
better medical provision, etc. By contrast, the National Women's
Aid Federation has always been more sensitive to the generally
oppressed position of women and in particular to the many factors
which make it very difficult for women to leave the man who batters
her and start a new life. Lack of adequate nursery provision,
women's poor earning power, the financial and legal dependence of
married women on their husbands, low levels of Supplementary Benefit,
extreme difficulties in finding accommodation, are all factors which
make women powerless against male violence, and are ongoing problems
which dog all women who are trying to make a new start.

For refuges that are hard pressed and struggling to keep going,
campaigning around these issues presents great problems, but at an
immediate level to provide help and support for women who are leaving
the refuges, questions about the amount of local nursery provision,
finding jobs, getting training, are all crucial. We cannot say that
we have really 'helped' battered women if after being in a refuge
they have to face several years of dependence on Supplementary
Benefit, bringing up children alone, on a soulless housing estate
often away from family and friends, but it is at this level that
local refuges may be able to raise in the community, among organisations active in the community, the oppressed reality of many women's
lives and to campaign for a woman's right to adequate child care,
housing and well-paid work.

Whether Women's Aid will develop along these lines remains to be
seen. If it is to do so it will need to keep constantly in mind the
reality that underlies this seemingly special problem - the reality
of women's objective position within the family, and that family
as a structure supported by the state. Women, when they are alone,
may be defined as unpersons by the state (for example, statistics of
the homeless do not even count those women who are attached, even if
it is just for one night, to a man). If they have children, they
immediately confront the state who will, in defining them as mothers,
at once make judgments about their capacities and worthiness.
Ultimately the challenge of Women's aid is not just that it demands
better and more liberal or more flexible state provision, nor is it
that it provides alternative structures in which women can live
their lives. This definition of feminism merely creates ghettos
within a hostile sexist society. The challenge of Women's Aid is
that it demands a fundamental change in the way in which women are
defined.

Notes

1 'Daily Express', 21 April 1975 (reply by Mme Giroud, France's
   Minister for Women's Affairs, to letter from Erin Pizzey).
2 Select Committee on Violence in Marriage (appointed by the House
   of Commons, 11 February 1975).
3 Penguin, 1974.
4 J.S. Mill, Protection of women, 'The Sunday Times', 24 August
   1851, p.2.

5   'North British Review', 25, May 1856, p.240.
6   ibid., pp.249-50.
7   Françoise Basch, 'Relative Creatures: Victorian Women in
    Society and the Novel: 1837-67', Allen Lane, 1974, pp.47-52.
    I am indebted to this work for the previous nineteenth-century
    references.
8   G. Stedman Jones, 'Outcast London', Oxford University Press,
    1971.
9   F.P. Cobbe, 'Life', London, Bentley, 1894, vol. 2, pp.220-1.
10 A. Wier, The reproduction of labour power, 'Case Con', spring
    1974.
11 E. Wilson, A Social Worker's Viewpoint, paper presented to the
    Royal Society of Health, 25 September 1975.
12 Report of the Committee on One-Parent Families, HMSO, July 1974.
13 Pizzey, op. cit., pp.9-11.
14 'Battered Women need Refuges', NWAF, 1975
15 ibid., p.31.
16 ibid., p.32.
17 ibid.
18 ibid., p.42.
19 'North Wales Chronicle', 17 April 1975.
20 Report from the Select Committee on Violence in Marriage, HMSO,
    30 July 1975, pp.298, 301.
21 Trades Union Congress Women's Conference, 14 March 1975.
22 National Union of Townswomen's Guilds, 21 May 1975.
23 National Federation of Women's Institutes, 4 June 1975.
24 Battered Women need Refuges', p.2.
25 ibid., p.11.
26 ibid., p.46.
27 Report ... on Violence in Marriage, p.2.
28 J.J. Gayford, Wife battering: a preliminary survey of 100 cases,
    'British Medical Journal', i, 1975, pp.194-7; Ten types of
    battered women, 'The Welfare Officer', 25 (1), 1976, pp.5-9.

12 Women and community work

Ann Gallagher

INTRODUCTION

In the past decade there has been a growing awareness of the need to
organize for social change in working-class communities.   The
importance of working in such communities has arisen from an understanding of the role of residents as consumers of social welfare,
defined broadly to include, for example, housing, education, public
amenities. (1)   In a welfare state, the 'notion of class must be
widened to include control of and access to the public services.'
(2)   If the community is another arena, alongside the work-place,
for the struggle for social change, it is also, in a particular
sense, the domain of women.   It refers to the 'round of life' for
which women are traditionally responsible, especially in industrial-
ized urban settings in which home and work are often quite separate.
The community ought to be the arena in which women's struggle
against oppression can find full expression.   But in many cases, the
roles women have played in community action are the familiar background and supporting parts, or leading roles in exclusively women's
groups which underline women's position in the family, for example
the 'mums' group'.
  To suggest that the community ought to be a major arena for women
is not to suggest that women should turn their attention exclusively
to community work and avoid the industrial struggle.   R. Farr offers
a note of caution here, 'The community, although an important field
of struggle largely ignored by traditional Marxists must not be seen
as an exclusively or predominately female battlefield.   This serves
only to institutionalize the division - capitalistically created - between men as waged, and the women as totally or partially unwaged.' (3)
Whereas the community should not be an exclusively female battlefield, or the only battlefield women fight on, it ought to be a
battlefield in which women are holding their own.
  This paper will discuss the part played by women in community
development.   It will consider the situations in working-class
communities in which women come together in significant numbers and
have influence in community groups, and when they are in the minority
or in the background; it will offer possible explanations for the
ways in which women participate in the community and examine the

121

implications of this participation for community workers and for
the women themselves. It will then consider the particular
situation of women community workers.

I will be writing mainly from my own experience and the experience of a variety of community groups in south-east London, and will
be discussing the roles played by women in developments in their
local areas.

THE PARTICIPATION OF WOMEN IN COMMUNITY GROUPS

What does community development and community action mean for women
in an age when the women's movement is, to say the least, a significant reality? Two pictures emerge. To a great extent, in working-
class areas where community development has flourished and a range
of new groups are active, the position of women in relation to men
remains essentially unchanged. On the other hand, in certain kinds
of deprived neighbourhoods and faced with particular issues, it is
the women who have come together and engaged in effective action.
Both of these situations have implications for community workers,
and especially for women community workers.

I want first to consider the situation in slightly better-off
working-class areas - post-war estates, many general improvement
areas - where respectability is an important aspect of people's
sense of themselves. In these localities the role of women in community development seems to be simply an extension of women's role in
society. Men are the leaders and prominent members of those groups
which have most influence in their immediate locality, that is groups
in which the leadership is involved in negotiating with other organisations, with councillors and officers, and in overseeing sizeable
grants, and even employing workers. In short, women, consistently,
have less influence in groups which have credibility and status.

In 1970 the situation on a new estate in Deptford, the northern
part of Lewisham, provided a clear example. In the opinion of the
local people the estate was the most desirable in that area of Lewisham at the time. The local Social Services office had contact with
a surprisingly small number of residents in relation to the size of
the estate. The tenants' association was strong and influential
with the local authority. It was financially well off, since it
successfully and regularly collected subscriptions from a good percentage of its large population. The association had a committee
of fourteen, all men. On the evenings that the men held meetings
in the committee room to discuss the business of the estate, the
women, many of them their wives, held sessions concerned with figure
and weight control in the downstairs hall.

Happily, situations in which sex roles are so clearly divided
seem to be less common now. But a consideration of community groups
in north Lewisham will show that the degree of participation by
women is still discouraging. On the newest estate in the area, the
activity of women in various groups reflects a familiar pattern.
Toward the end of 1974, as the last of the arriving tenants settled
into their new homes, the tenants' association was strong and vital.
A number of committees were functioning somewhat independently, but
were co-ordinated by a main committee. This main committee was the

most influential group on the estate. Men comprised more than half
its members, but women were present and active. The offices of
chairman, vice-chairman, and treasurer were held by men, while the
secretary was a woman. On the sub-committees, the chairman of the
adventure playground committee (which received a reasonably large
grant from the council), the newsletter committee, the community
centre committee (the association had fought for, and won, control
of this facility) were men. The main committee and the playground
committee had women secretaries. Women chaired the playgroup and
entertainments committees. This is a typical example of women's
participation. Women are usually involved, but in a slight minority
in the more influential groups. If a strong woman holds a position,
it is probably that of secretary. In the north-west part of the
borough there are ten active tenants' associations of varying sizes
which are well organized and which meet together periodically. In
all these associations a man holds the position of chairman, but in
no less than seven out of the ten a woman is the secretary and/or
social secretary.

Neighbourhood groups can exert some influence beyond their
immediate locality through co-ordinating bodies which bring together
a number of groups and associations under one umbrella. However, it
is difficult for women to move into significant roles in these.
There is a great deal of anxiety, especially in the early stages,
when separate groups agree to come together and co-operate.
Understandably, when sending representatives to a federated effort,
each group is concerned that its voice be equal to all others. The
individual organizations are giving up a measure of autonomy and if
other member groups are much stronger than they, they will be in
the position of followers. If men have played more forceful roles
in their respective groups, they will go forward to these umbrella
organizations. Representation on the local community association,
a federation of tenants' and residents' groups, demonstrates this
point. Of the nine member groups, seven are represented by men
only; one is represented by a man and a woman, and only one by a
woman alone. The chairman is male and the secretary female.

A seven-year-old federation, a neighbourhood council, consists of
neighbourhood groups and associations active mainly in the area of
the borough west and south of Deptford. The neighbourhood council
has considerable influence both in the immediate area and the borough
as a whole and employs its own staff. Only six of the twenty-six
members of the executive committee, some of whom are sent from their
respective groups and some of whom are elected at large at the Annual
General Meeting, are women.

Certainly women in these areas are often conscious of the lower
expectations of them. One extremely capable woman was nominated by
a tenants' association for election to a borough-wide committee on
play facilities. Only after the elections did the association realise that in fact the committee she had been elected to was a joint
body comprising mainly chairmen of council committees with an equal
number of representatives from voluntary organizations, and that
the committee had considerable influence over funding and other
matters. She was certain that if the importance of the committee
had been realized beforehand, one of the men from the association
would have gone forward instead.

There are, of course, exceptions. One woman is both the
secretary to the community association, and is also chairwoman
of the borough federation of tenants' and residents' associations.
But the consistency with which men are the formal leaders, and the
part women play in the everyday workings of neighbourhood groups,
reflects the subordinate position of women in society.

WOMEN'S GROUPS

In these neighbourhoods there are situations in which women are in
leadership positions, but these are none the less restricting. They
are groups which generally consist entirely of women - mums' groups,
mothers' meeting around pre-school playgroups, mothers' and toddlers'
groups, one o'clock clubs. (Youth clubs and adventure playground
committees may also be women's groups, but these are more likely
to include men. As children get older and as playgrounds receive
grants, each becomes less exclusively women's business.) These
groups understandably attract only or mainly women because they are
concerned essentially with children or with the isolation of women
at home with children. In addition, social or entertainment clubs
and committees frequently consist entirely, or almost entirely, of
women, extending woman's role of hostess into community activity.
    At present these groups, which might be considered 'traditional
women's groups', play a crucial role because they reach and bring
together numbers of women who might otherwise be desperate in their
loneliness or isolation. They also give parents some influence
over facilities for their children. But it is important to question
whether or not they merely provide women with limited outlets which
are consistent with a conventional view of woman as wife and mother.
Are women drawn into these groups, rather than given a real opportunity to participate in the more 'serious business' of the tenants'
or neighbourhood associations? Here we need to look at the part
played by community workers. Do workers too readily decide to work
toward setting up, and encouraging women to join, these traditional
women's groups? Does the worker say too quickly, 'And maybe we
can have something in the afternoon for the "mums"'? The term
'mums' group' could stifle creative exploration of different opportunities and reinforce women's sense of themselves as people dependent
on others for their identity. It may too readily convey to them
the impression that the worker considers these groups their form of
participation while the men take decisions about the area, negotiate
with the council, and so on.
    An interesting development on a large new south-east London
estate illustrates this point. A 'mothers' group' had been in
existence and meeting regularly for nine months. Some of their husbands became interested as they had little contact with other people
on the estate. Gradually the group became a parents' association
and began meeting in the evenings. Shortly after this development,
the group took a competitive interest in the tenants' association.
They publicly expressed the view that the tenants' association was
not doing its job - did not reach the people - and urged tenants
to join the parents' association instead. A period of tension followed until a delegation from the parents' association was

was invited to the tenants' association meeting. A male delegation
attended, and hostility between the two groups ceased. The
tenants' association invited a member of the parents' association
to sit on its committee, and one of the men was chosen. I am con-
vinced that it would not have occurred to the 'mothers' group to
see themselves in the same light as the tenants' association and
they certainly would not have considered issuing a challenge. When
men joined the group, the group could look outside, at least to the
immediate environment, and take some action in this area.

Groups explicitly for women who are at home with children often
restrict themselves to domestic issues and circumscribe women's
activity along these lines. One of the serious dangers in this is
that women may 'underperform'. The context of the group can be
pervasive and women may become confined to a stereotype instead of
being to some extent liberated by the experience of the group.
As a worker at The Albany, a south-east London settlement, I was
responsible for bringing together a group of young women on their
own with children. They met regularly to discuss their common
experiences and difficulties. The group was pleasant, at times
lively, and occasionally agreed on some corporate action. But, on
the whole, the members concerned themselves in a fairly surface way
with domestic matters - the children, housework, shopping, boyfriends.

After this group had been meeting for some months, several of us
who were connected with the settlement started a women's group.
This consisted of several local women who were active in the South-
East London Claimants' Union and other activities in The Albany,
and included some of the staff, several 'professional' women, and
two of the single mothers from the group mentioned above. The
experience of the group was exciting for all of us. At that time
there was a concern in the women's movement that working-class
women might be alienated from the movement, in part, because they
did not identify with small groups involved in 'consciousness-
raising', and this was for many women the starting-point of involvement. In this situation we found that working-class and middle-
class women could sit alongside each other, sharing, responding to,
and valuing each other's very different experiences. The most
impressive, and also worrying, aspect of the group for me was the
performance of the two young women from the mothers' group. In the
women's group they became intense and vital people with a number of
complex feelings about their situations. One of these mothers described,with a great deal of detail and sensitivity, giving birth in
hospital as a young woman on her own. They both exhibited an awareness which had not come out in the young mothers' group. I felt
that there was something about the setting of the mothers' group
which stifled the potential of the women and encouraged them to
perform according to certain expectations. A sensitive worker might
bring out in the mothers' group what came out in the women's group.
Unfortunately this does not happen to any great extent. Too often
the 'mums' group' atmosphere is a handicap, and risks being a device
for the containment of women.

In making this criticism I do not wish to decry the obvious value
of these groups. The activities of the groups are important in
themselves, and through them women pick up skills and confidence.

These groups are often the only outlet for women and may provide a
way to start 'where people are'. There are examples of groups of
women who have made such starts and moved to broader areas of
influence. This is true in the case of co-ordinating and federated
organizations mentioned above. These enable some women to move
from traditional women's groups to a more influential organization.

Criticism of traditional women's groups also risks undervaluing
the importance of day care provision for children. A number of
these women's groups are concerned with pre-school playgroups,
child-minding and nursery provision. While this is left to the
women as a relatively minor concern, it is nevertheless crucial
to women and to children.

It is important, also, not to lose sight of the importance for
women of having the opportunity of meeting alone, even if the
particular groups in which they meet sometimes seem to limit them.
Women may need to develop confidence in whatever women's setting is
available in order to be able to move into other areas. Interestingly, a mothers' and toddlers' group which has been meeting on a
south-east London estate for some time is now beginning to look at
women's issues and discuss them from women's perspectives. Because
women were meeting alone, this development was possible.

WHY WOMEN'S PARTICIPATION IS LIMITED

In order that women and community workers can begin to grapple with
the constraints on women's participation, it is necessary to consider why these constraints exist. Several explanations have been
looked at, indirectly at least, so far. Others are there by implication and need to be considered more fully.

1. If working-class women consider themselves well off because
of their husbands, and gain respect for their position in relation
to him, they may not wish to challenge the role women play at home,
in the community or at work. The situation of women in male-
dominated community groups is no worse than in other areas in
society. It is just not better. If the woman is not concerned and
actively trying to change the position of women in a number of areas,
it is unlikely that she will make an exception of a tenants'
association.

2. Many women lack the confidence to plunge into tenants'
associations run by men and are happy to find involvement in a
women's group.

3. Women with small children often have difficulty in attending
evening meetings. Since the men are more likely to be available in
the evening, the more influential groups meet at that time.

4. Some women face serious difficulties in becoming involved in
groups with a number of men because their partners are threatened
by this. Like the woman, the man may feel vulnerable in his own
right. He may be trapped in an uninspiring job and feel that home
is the only respite, the only place in which he is in some control.
He may be afraid to lose this. It is acceptable, from his point of
view, if his wife joins with other women in a variety of activities,
but he might object when she is involved with men in groups. He
might be unhappy, too, at being deprived of certain domestic
services if his wife begins to commit time outside the home.

WHEN WOMEN BECOME ACTIVE

All of these constraints and difficulties might lead us to believe
that there is limited potential for women in community efforts.
But in certain neighbourhoods there is considerable potential in
women's involvement. We need to ask where women appear in significant numbers and in the forefront of community groups. In my
experience, women are more likely to be in the forefront of
community activity in various groups in more seriously deprived
areas. By more seriously deprived I mean areas of greater poverty,
with more run-down housing, areas which are, in general, less
socially respectable than the neighbouring locality. In these
settings women are capable of performing in a number of ways incon-
sistent with the female stereotype. I would like to illustrate
this with three examples of groups which have been active in
Deptford.

EXAMPLE 1: THE CROSSFIELD CAMPAIGN

Crossfield Estate is an old estate in Deptford. It was considered
a 'problem estate' by much of officialdom, and by community people
from surrounding areas. Crossfield referrals to the local Social
Services office, resulting from material poverty, were four times
the average for the local area. (4) Most Crossfield tenants felt
strongly about the substandard housing conditions on the estate and
believed that the Greater London Council and now the local authority
had deserted them. The estate was becoming more and more run down.
'We are part of society and we are not getting our fair share', was
the opinion of many tenants.
    In January 1973, in connection with a GLC road-widening scheme,
Lewisham planned to knock down the blocks on the estate which
fronted on the street, but leave a number of blocks on an 'island',
surrounded by a four-lane carriageway, Deptford Creek, and the
railway. A 1972 GLC report said, 'the Estate would remain permanently severed from shopping, schools and open spaces ... to bring
the [properties] within Wilson standards would require fixed double
glazing and mechanical ventilation.' (5) Conditions on the estate,
hardly tolerable, would become unbearable.
    In response to this situation, the women on the estate rose in
opposition. Of about 200 people who participated in the campaign
which followed, about 170 were women. The hard core of active people
numbered 32, and six of these were men.
    Once this group was mobilized, they acted with an unusual amount
of energy and commitment. I think this was because the women felt
they had little left to lose. As one tenant said: 'I've lived on
this estate for twenty-two years; I have spent twenty-one years
trying to get out.' It was also because a great deal of anger
finally found expression. When the Chief Housing Officer, the Deputy
Town Clerk, and several local councillors walked out of the first
mass meeting in the campaign after half an hour (to attend a meeting
on a better-off estate (6)), the room, overcrowded anyway, exploded
with the pent-up anger of over 125 people. Women were on their feet
shouting at their elected representatives and the public servants to

stop and listen. The official entourage ignored this warning and
left. After this, people's anger turned to a commitment to action.
A co-ordinating committee of eighteen women and four men was chosen.

In the course of the following two months, Crossfield women took
the lead in a number of areas which are generally left to the men
on other estates. They held small and large meetings to mobilize
support and to demonstrate the strength of feeling on the estate.
They circulated petitions; arranged for small groups to put their
case directly to local councillors and for a larger group to lobby
their MP at Westminster and, with some fanfare and publicity, got
him to inspect the conditions on the estate.

Together with staff of The Albany, the women produced an effective propaganda document and held a press conference to launch it.
A woman chaired the conference, giving a short but quotable speech,
and replying to various questions concerning the document.

Crossfield women were also able to take direct and disruptive
action. This is something which many active community groups find
difficult, or do not consider, because it falls outside their particular style of operating. Crossfield tenants staged a demonstration
closing the 'to-be-widened' road to traffic during the rush hour on
a Friday evening - in the midst of a rail strike! They undertook
the demonstration with relative ease in spite of the fact that women
are supposed to be more conforming and accommodating than men. (7)
The tenants were able both to work with their supporters from
the council, mainly the chairman of the Planning Committee and one
local councillor, and also to confront opposition. Finally, on
21 March the Housing Committee agreed to rehouse all the tenants on
the estate.

The significance of the Crossfield campaign here is that consistently, throughout the campaign, women were in leading positions. In
most of the activities that took place throughout the two months
from large meetings to small groups visiting a councillor, women
represented about four-fifths of the group. The two offices of
chairman and secretary were held by women. (Interestingly, a young
man on the estate assisted the chairman by co-chairing the large
meetings with council officials.)

EXAMPLE 2:   HOMELESS FAMILIES ACTION COMMITTEE

A group of ex-homeless families who came together to pressure for
improvements in their slum properties provide an interesting example
of a small group of women in the forefront of community action.

Background

In Lewisham, homeless families receive better treatment than in a
number of other local authorities. But of course, this is not much
of a commendation. Homeless families are housed in short-life, often
substandard, property for a 'temporary' period which may be as long
as seven years. They are given the impression that they are not
proper council tenants; they are considered to be 'problem families'
and have special rent books. When they prove they are 'good tenants'

by keeping a tidy house and having a 'clean rent book' (no arrears) for a period of time, they are considered deserving of council tenant status and will be considered for rehousing.

A number of social workers in the Social Services Department, where I was employed as a community worker, and a social worker from a voluntary organization found that they had been continually pressing for the rehousing of some families for up to five years. We realized that the families were particular vulnerable because they were unorganized, and we therefore agreed to bring them together. In June 1974, a few women attended a meeting and talked about the effect on their children of the conditions in which they lived. They described the humiliating treatment they received at the Homeless Families Unit when they complained about their houses. In one case, when a woman called in at the Unit to press to be rehoused, a housing officer phoned the employment exchange and arranged a job for her husband! The job paid less than the man was able to claim from Social Security. Nothing was done about the housing. On another occasion a woman on her own with eight children was told she would be considered for rehousing when she paid her £55 rent arrears. This woman's sister gave her the £55. On learning that the sister had paid the arrears, the homeless family officer said the payment did not really count as she had not managed to clear the debt herself! He none the less took the money. One woman put the case clearly: 'You are made to feel an outcast just because you have once been homeless. The council calls us problem families, but where is the problem? The problem is housing, isn't it?' Most of the women had friends in similar situations who they felt would be interested in the group. It was agreed that we would try to involve more ex-homeless families. We also discussed pressurizing local councillors and chief officers to take some action. We talked about the Public Health Inspector as a council employee and decided to ask the help of the Independent Public Health Authority Service (PHAS). The women were pessimistic about achieving anything, but were willing to try. 'Things couldn't get any worse.'

One of the interesting aspects of this experience was the involvement of a variety of workers. Three social workers, a community worker and a community work student joined the women at the initial meeting. This could have meant too many workers, but because each of the social workers came with one of the five women, and the community workers were working in the area, relationships were comfortable. I think the women were surprised and encouraged that other ex-homeless families were as frustrated as they, and that a number of people were concerned about their situation.

By the next meeting the tenants, now seven women and a man, were feeling more optimistic. We arranged for PHAS to do independent inspections on several properties. The group agreed to produce an information leaflet with photographs exposing the appalling housing conditions, and tentatively planned to meet local councillors.

By the third meeting, PHAS had visited three houses, written long reports on the badly needed repairs and had told us that the properties were in such bad condition that tenants could take court action against Lewisham borough council under Section 99 of the 1936 Public Health Act. The information that the council was guilty of infringing their rights had a special value for these families,

since they were consistently made to feel guilty about having been
homeless and about living in substandard housing. Not only did this
information clarify the fact that the families were not the problem,
it also gave them a much needed weapon. The group, now consisting
of ten women and two men, were apprehensive but hopeful. They
involved a local Citizens' Advice Bureau solicitor, and began to put
their case to the council, threatening legal action by individual
families if their situations were not improved. Several families
were rehoused after these threats. Then things came to a standstill,
and it became clear that the group would have to proceed to court.
A great deal of anxiety surrounded the action, as members of the
action committee felt very vulnerable. They still depended upon the
council for their housing and feared reprisals. However, it was
clear that the women had gained strength through the group, had
become more militant and angry about their situation, and were
ready to go to court. On the other hand some of the husbands who
had not been involved in the activity were anxious, and began to
discourage their wives from taking action. One would simply not
allow his wife to take out a summons. Finally one woman led a small
group to Camberwell Court and took out a summons against the
borough. There was no need to take the case to court, since she
was rehoused well before the date of the court hearing. In subsequent months all ten families were rehoused.

EXAMPLE 3: SOUTH-EAST LONDON CLAIMANTS' UNION

The early history of the South-East London Claimants' Union provides
an example of a large group in which a man was in the most influential position, but women were present in numbers and influence.

Background

The Claimants' Union was established by a young male claimant with
the help of Albany staff in the summer of 1971. After a short time
twenty to thirty claimants attended weekly meetings, and the union
was successful in representing a number of people at local Social
Security offices. During this early phase the union attracted a
good number of local claimants who had no previous experience of
community activity, although some of them had been active in trade
unions. Women with children comprised about three-quarters of this
membership. Together with the man who helped initiate the union and
who was the key figure in the group, women played significant roles,
frequently winning victories at the 'SS', staffing the Claimants'
Union office and recruiting new members. When a struggle over the
leadership of the group erupted between two men, it was the women who
effectively held the union together. By December 1971 the women were
eager to take some action on their own. They staged a women's demonstration in the local Social Security office, refusing to leave until
they received £7.50 extra for Christmas for each person in the
family. Eventually, they were carried from the Social Security
office by the police. (The women did not receive extra money, but
several gained enough confidence to spend all of their two-week

Christmas payment in one week and then present themselves at the
office, penniless with a week ahead of them. In these cases the
women received extra grants.) In the case of the Claimants'
Union, unlike Crossfield and the homeless families action committee,
women were able to hold their own and occasionally take independent
militant action in an organization in which men, though a
considerable minority, were in key positions.

There are other examples of women taking the lead in community
action. Jalna Hanmer and Hilary Rose state that it is 'empirically
readily observable that the most militant strata in both claimants'
unions and squatting are women with dependent children unsupported
by men.'(8)

'Spare Rib' reports on the action of women in Liverpool when the
city council decided to raise council rents by up to £2 a week. (9)
The properties which had the biggest increases were mainly inner-city
tenements and tower blocks, and old walk-ups - the worst housing there.

> Throughout the summer ... women tenants in particular have been
> protesting against the condition in which they have to live.
> When rents went up in June tenants took action. They've been on
> rent strike, demonstrated and occupied the housing offices to
> force the Council to take notice of their demands.
>   Most of the people who came to the meetings and demonstra-
> tions were kids and women ... Many women were angry that they
> did not get more support from the men ... the men aren't inter-
> ested. There'd be more of them at the meetings if they were.

WHY WOMEN BECOME ACTIVE IN POORER NEIGHBOURHOODS

Why is it that women seem to come to the fore in these more desperate situations? Is there a latent reserve that is only tapped
by a sense of urgency about the family's survival? Is there a
potential that is rarely developed?

A number of factors may help to explain why women are prominent
in community action based on crucial issues in deprivation situations.

1. According to the Merseyside Big Flame Womens' Group, meetings
and demonstrations involved mostly kids and women because they
'have to bear the brunt of bad conditions'. (10) Women suffer more
immediately and directly from poor housing conditions. Poor conditions prevent them from doing good work as mothers, as the ex-
homeless families action committee members clearly stated in their
publicity leaflets:

> 'It's conditions like this that make children leave home. My
> teenage daughter is threatening to leave because she is too
> ashamed to bring her friends home.'

> 'The mice run over the children's faces in the night. My baby's
> face has been covered in bites and my little boy is under the
> doctor for nerve rash because he is so frightened.'

Women are continually worried about their children in these neighbourhoods and generally deal with the police, courts, and social
workers when children get into trouble. Also a woman becomes
desperate about poverty when it means she cannot buy food and pay

the rent. The home is the woman's only situation. The men may
get some relief from their world outside the immediate locality,
even if it is more of a change than a rest.

2. A man, on the other hand, may be more humiliated by the
conditions in which his family is forced to live than the woman.
He is the breadwinner; his job is to provide for the family. Unless
he has a clear perspective on his position, the man probably internalizes his situation and feels that he has failed. Man's
relationship to status is relevant here. 'Except in special circumstances, a woman derives her status from the man to whom she is
attached while a man derives his own status.' (11) If he 'comes
out' as a tenant on a particular estate or as a 'homeless family',
he risks being labelled and further publicizing this perceived
'failure'. He may need to preserve a different image of himself,
especially if he has separate worlds - work, the pub where he
drinks - in short, settings in which he is a different person.
An indication of this as a significant factor is the vehemence with
which men urge their 'active' wives to avoid publicity, saying, for
example, 'Just don't get your name in the paper.'

3. Women's 'borrowed status' may help to explain why women in
certain situations can take fairly militant action. Women whose
husbands are providing for them may be more willing to undertake,
and even be more committed to, a somewhat traditional role for
women. If they wish to be active, they are satisfied to be active
in women's groups and in the background in other groups. If a
woman's 'borrowed status' is not valued, and she feels she has
little to lose in her situation, she may be more likely to break
out of traditional constraints and rebel against her situation.
In the early stages of the ex-homeless families action committee,
women were not hopeful, but said things such as: 'Might as well
try this. Nothing else has worked.' The Claimants' Union women
who were dragged from the SS office by the police did not in any way
feel that they had a great deal to lose by placing themselves in such
a compromising situation. They felt it was time they took a stand.

4. We know that oppressed people continue to be oppressed to a
great extent because they identify with the values of their oppress-
ors and thus help to support the system which defends these values.
When an event or intervention enables people to redefine their situation, to see themselves as victims of unfair conditions rather than
guilty in a fair situation, they can rebel against the values and the
system which serves them so badly. For the women in Crossfield,
the homeless action committee and in the Claimants' Union, coming
together to consider their situation corporately released a great
deal of anger and led to a clearer perception of themselves as hard
done by and not as inadequate. This made it possible for them to
rebel. It also made it possible to take what was from their point
of view fairly dramatic action against the existing situation.
Perhaps it also helped them to break out of the traditional women's
role. Robin Morgan points out: 'Every time drastic change has
shaken the established social order, some drive for women's rights
has surfaced ... There's something contagious about demanding freedom.' (12) Perhaps there's something contagious and pervasive
about taking action against the established order. If you can begin
to question and challenge the local bureaucracy, it may become easier
to break out of other areas of social conditioning.

5. Another reason why women were more involved is undoubtedly
the fact that more women were suffering from the situations with
which the groups were concerned: e.g. Crossfield had a high proportion of women on their own with children, and a large number of
claimants are unsupported mothers.

6. The way in which a group of action begins may play a part in
determining who joins. The fact that both the Crossfield campaign
and the action committee started with small groups of women may
have 'fixed' the activity as something the women were doing, and
discouraged men from joining.

7. A factor which this article does not fully explore is the sex
of the worker. In the three examples provided in some detail, I was
involved as a community worker, although other workers were also
involved in the homeless families action committee. Would a man
working in these situations have produced different results?

IMPLICATIONS OF WOMEN'S PARTICIPATION

Throughout this article, I have presented two pictures. One is that
in working-class area, where community development has flourished
and there are many active groups, the position of women in relation
to men in such groups does not deviate from women's traditional
position in society.

The second picture is that in neighbourhoods of severe deprivation, women come together, engage in effective community action
and act in ways which are not consistent with stereotypes of
women.

Each of these pictures represents a situation in which community
work has a particular task in relation to women. In the first picture, in community development settings in which women play more
traditional roles, the task is clear although it is not simple - in
fact it is extremely difficult. What needs to be done is evident
and is similar to the ways in which women need to support each other
in a number of settings. In this case I would like to offer some
fairly straightforward suggestions for community work practice. The
task in areas of poverty is far less clear because it raises
questions which strike at the core of community work in relation to
inequality and oppression. In this case, I would like to pin-point
some of the issues, questions and work implications which arise from
the task. I think it is the responsibility of all community workers
to contribute where they can to both these undertakings; more particularly, it is the responsibility of women community workers, since
their stake in the outcome of this work is, in the long run, as great
as that of the women with whom they are working.

The first picture reflects the situation in which we women generally find ourselves. We play the supporting, not the leading, parts.
We comply with the stereotypes of women as more 'receptive', 'passive', 'nurturing' and giving. We consent to the stereotype of men
as more 'active', more 'dominant', more inclined toward 'leadership'. (13) The qualities women are expected to possess are not
negative, but we are expected to possess them in combinations which
keep us from interfering with male leadership.

In these traditional women's groups good community work means

helping women to move within the setting of the group. This involves listening for and supporting interest in areas which will help
women to grow, to discover and look at new ideas, to be aware of
the potential within themselves, to consider their position as
women and as mothers, to look at and act on social issues. It
means working in such a way that women's groups offer the possibili-
ties that The Albany group offered the young mothers when the
'mums' group' remained static. Women in male-dominated groups need
special support in order to perform as equals. The worker can help
women to reflect on and to learn from their participation; to look
at their contribution to groups and how these contributions are
received; to be aware when men are not listening - dismissing their
ideas before hearing them; to be aware of their own tendency to
underrate women's contributions. At the same time, the worker
needs to help women to understand male resistance, to understand
the social pressures and conditioning which make it difficult for
men to give up their leading position or to see women as equals.
Without this understanding, the women may eventually become resent-
ful about the situation and give up.

The second picture indicates that there is a particular potential
for organizing women for action in disadvantaged communities around
certain issues. Women in these areas experience certain forms of
oppression as women. Women in the Claimants' Union, raising children
on their own, were oppressed with poverty for having children and
having lost, or never had, a man to support them. They were consistently humiliated when they attempted to attain the means to
provide for their children themselves. In spite of the dramatic
and well publicized housing shortage, people without houses are
made to feel guilty. Women in homeless families generally deal with
the housing officials, and bear the brunt of this emotional bullying.

Women living in run-down neighbourhoods with poor and overcrowded
housing, with numbers of children and limited facilities, cannot
raise their children as they would like. We know that certain kinds
of environments produce greater incidences of juvenile crime. Yet
mothers are continually blamed when their children get into trouble.
We know, at least we women know, that it is extremely difficult both
physically and psychologically to keep a substandard dwelling 'clean
and tidy'. And yet women are punished for not doing this by being
refused rehousing or, if the authority wants to knock down their
dwelling, being given another substandard house.

Having thus deprived women of resources and humiliated them,
society offers them social workers. And frequently, though not
always, the social worker compounds the oppression by confirming,
simply by reason of role, that the woman's difficulties stem from
her own inadequacy. These women might accurately paraphrase Malcolm
X and say, 'The worst thing the welfare state has done is to teach us
to hate ourselves.' (14) It is this situation - women experiencing
material and psychological oppression as women, brought face to face
with social workers, the majority of whom at this level are women -
which raises a serious challenge to the women's movement. Why has
there been no alliance between the two groups? Why at a time when
the women's movement is influencing all of us, has this situation
not been viewed in terms of sisterhood? Elizabeth Wilson says: (15)

Most social workers in the field are still women; and most
of their clients are women. The casework relationship, as it
commonly works out, simply serves to divide the two groups.
Far from showing solidarity with clients, workers often pity
and patronise them for their ill success in managing their men,
money and children.

Community workers have tended to stay away from these women as
well. While it is true that there are theoretical differences between community work and social work, I think community workers have
been so anxious to assert that they are not social workers that they
resist working in areas where people are 'not coping'. In their
struggle to be free of social work, community workers risk wanting
to be free of the most disadvantaged. This is a little like saying,
'I'm a revolutionary. I don't want to be bothered about the
oppressed!'

Perhaps the conflicts are not just theoretical? What might be
operating here to some extent is that social work, in spite of
Seebohm, large salaries, high-level posts and more men, is still
considered a female profession. It involves caring, empathy,
support. Community work is more aggressive, involving action, conflict, change. More male? Does some of the community work disdain
for social work come from the anxiety of men in a 'male profession'
- community work - which may be dwarfed and swallowed up in a
'female profession' - social work? Are the men saying that a community worker is not a caring person; a community worker is a radical activist? Male not female. If this is so, the task falls to
women community workers to seek the balance.

We women who are community workers can begin to show solidarity
with oppressed women in the community. To do this we must address
ourselves to injustices which women feel most keenly. We will need
consciously to work in such a way that women have the opportunity to
channel their frustration into effective action. Maybe we can
encourage women social workers to join us. Too often they have only
been able to help other women to 'cope' with frustration. Perhaps
most importantly, we need to be aware that the anger and courage of
women in these communities is a potential force for women and for
change.

OBSTACLES FOR WOMEN IN ORGANIZING FOR CHANGE

With the hope that women community workers may begin a more concerted effort on behalf of women in the communities in which they work,
it may be useful to look at some of the difficulties women face in
struggles for change.

With any oppressed group there are likely to be effects of oppression which must be overcome or at least taken into account in
order that the group can come together and be effective. In the
early 1960s, in the midst of the US civil rights movement, a black
psychiatrist wrote an article called 'Black roadblocks to Black
unity'. (16) In it he looked at the difficulties black people faced
in organizing for power because of their experience of oppression;
e.g. undervaluing and distrust of each other. We need to consider
'roadblocks' or obstacles which women face in organizing for change.

Women tend to underrate themselves and other women. We do not take each other seriously. Real and important matters involve men. We look to men for opinions and standards. We measure our intelligence by male respect and approval. We listen in a different way to men and women.   Karen Horney says that a woman may have no faith in women's capacity for any real achievement and be rather inclined to identify with the masculine disregard for women. (17) In further support of this, recent studies of judgments of female competence show that men and women 'evaluate male performance and effectiveness more highly. Even in tasks which are traditionally female-appropriate, females are only rated as good as men.' (18)

This self-deprecation is obvious in the behaviour of women who represent traditional women's groups in a federated organization. Women who are articulate leaders in their own group often fall silent in a mixed-sex group. In groups in which men dominate, women will often accept questionable statements from men as fact, but will question the contributions of other women. Such a sense of inferiority can hamper a group of women who are challenging policies and government authorities usually represented by men. First of all the women may not appreciate the strengths and talents of themselves and other members of the group. After all they are just a bunch of women.

If women overvalue men's opinions and need male approval, they are more vulnerable to being persuaded or co-opted in negotiations with men. I worked with a group of poor white women in a midwestern city in the USA in the mid-1960s. Their main battle was with the public welfare department, in the person of a male director. Initially, women were forceful and demanding. They won a number of victories because of this. Although the women were demanding long overdue rights, the director yielded to them with an air of paternal concern. The women came to enjoy this benevolence. They slipped into the classic role of women relating to a man in a position of importance, and became ineffective in their negotiations with him.

Some women turn their frustration at being dominated by men against other women, (19) repeating a common tendency of oppressed people. When a strong woman is accepted as a leader she may carefully guard her hard-won position. She is often competitive toward other women who look like possible leaders. She strives to maintain her position with her new male reference group rather than to share the leadership with more women. Perhaps the internalizes the men's opinion of women.

Related to this, we women often rival each other instead of supporting each other. This occurred when a husband and wife team became active and began to bring together several antipathetic factions in their community. The woman did most of the day-to-day work, keeping people informed about what was going on, about the time and place of meetings, about what could be done with individual grievances. The man took charge at meetings and other public meetings, and was the chairman of the association. In spite of the fact that the man had the formal power, the women in the neighbourhood criticized his wife for thinking she was 'someone important' and for having a 'hand in everything'. The man received none of this criticism. It is difficult for women to move into leadership positions because other women will be embarrassed, jealous, and/or angered by this and try to push them back into their 'place'.

Many qualities needed by people engaged in community action are qualities which society cultivates or at least tolerates in men but discourages in women. We are conditioned to be more accommodating, dependent and receptive than men. (20) These qualities do not provide the basis for radical action. They can present diffi- culties to women in sustaining an unpopular position or in tough negotiating. The 'sociology of deviancy reserves a special place for women as being particularly conformist'. (21) It may there- fore be especially difficult for women to confront the opposition. Interestingly, this was not a serious problem with Crossfield women or with the Claimants' Union.

Women are not likely to be as experienced in groups and associa- tions as men. This can have some advantages. I have found that women are less likely, for example, to want to create elaborate organizational structures which end up excluding people. But it has disadvantages. Again the group may be more vulnerable in negotiating with officials if they can be baffled by procedures. Their own early stages may be less smooth and certainly less efficient than groups with more experienced members.

When women come together around specific issues, it is difficult for them to sustain action once the problem is resolved. Women can put aside other demands for a while and respond to an urgent situa- tion with a great deal of time and energy. But when the urgency is over, family demands usually have to take priority again. Workers will need to devise structures which can accommodate this type of involement. People do not need to be constantly 'active' as long as they identify with a group or organization which has some kind of permanence and to which they can turn for help, or respond to, as the need arises.

Women may be limited in their participation by their men. I have already mentioned that some men discourage their partners from participating in groups with other men, and some object to any loss of attention when women become active. This means that women's groups are vulnerable. They can lose crucial members at any time if domestic pressure becomes too great.

A man who does not object to either of the above situations may object to the woman's involvement in any form of challenging acti- vity, because he fears reprisals. One difficulty here is that he is not part of the group. If he has not gone through the processes leading up to the action, he is likely to be out of step with the group and therefore less likely to believe in the group's potential. Yet he has the final say. Should the worker try hard to encourage the men into the group in this case? They are suffering from the same material deprivation as the women, even if less intensely. An organization of women and men could be larger and stronger. Would this be possible. And if so, would it have a destructive effect on the group?

If the men do not join the group, the worker will need to support the women in their handling of men's objections.

WOMEN COMMUNITY WORKERS

Having considered some of the difficulties facing groups of women,
I would like to look at the situation for women community workers.
If we can accept that social conditioning affects women's behaviour,
then it seems to me that the effect of this conditioning facili-
tates community work in certain interesting ways. In other areas
the work may be more difficult for women.

The relationship of the community worker to the group has simi-
larities with the relationship between a woman and her family.
The worker is expected to be supportive, to develop the strengths
within the group rather than her own strengths. She should bring
out abilities and leadership qualities in others. This does not
mean that she should be passive or particularly non-directive.
It simply means, as with the conventional wife and mother,
that her self-interest rests firmly with the interest of others.
She derives her status from the success or failure of the group.
She measures her success in terms of the group's experience.
This is not the only approach to community work, but it is an
important one, and clearly the appropriate approach with certain
groups.

Because of the parallel between the role of a 'community worker'
and the role of 'wife and mother' into which women are socialized,
it may be easier for the woman worker to play down her role, to
allow the group to have its victories and its defeats rather than
claim them herself. It may be easier for her to lead from behind and
to derive her own reward from the experience of others.

On the other hand women may find it more difficult to perform
more aggressive 'male' parts - to engage in protest and confront
the opposition - when the situation calls for this. Confrontation
requires nonconformity, not being nice or pleasant, and women are
disposed to please. This may help the worker to avoid confrontation for its own sake. However, she must be sure, when avoiding
this approach, that it is the situation, not her own fear or dis-
comfort, which determines what she does. The decision must be a
tactical one which takes into account the consciousness of the group,
not the worker's own needs.

It is easier for a woman to play a background role with the
public and with officials. This can have tactical advantages.
Because men tend not to perceive a woman as a key and influential
person in a group, men who represent statutory or formal organizations will be less conscious of the woman worker than they would be
of a man. It will therefore be more difficult for them to dismiss
issues by convincing themselves that there is really no problem, but
that some community worker is stirring local agitation.

A woman worker is less likely to carry personal status than a male
worker. She is therefore more dependent on the resources and
strengths in the group. This may make her more conscious of the
group's anxieties and more intimately aware of the group's need for
solidarity. She needs this too.

There are, of course, disadvantages in having limited personal
status. The woman worker will not be taken as seriously as a man.
This can limit her effectiveness in manoeuvring within the Town Hall
and with other governing authorities, but it can also undercut her

effectiveness when taking a strong stand with a group. When I was
involved in a forcible ejection from a Social Security office, the
manager, whom I had met in a more respectable setting, said:
'I'm surprised to see someone like you involved in something like
this.' Almost, 'What's a nice girl ...'

It can be easier for a woman to avoid giving the impression that
she will take care of things, rather than work with the group to
get things done. People less readily expect a woman to produce the
goods. I recently disagreed with a male colleague about the value
of a worker making door-to-door contacts in a new area. He found
that this was not a useful approach for him because, once he had
visited people and discussed the neighbourhood, he was expected to
show some results. I have used this approach a number of times
and found it invaluable to future work. My difficult was very different from that of my male colleague. Having done a good deal of
listening and having found areas of common concern, my problem was
convincing people that something could be done.

On the other hand, women community workers may be more frequently
asked to act as social workers than men. Women are expected to
empathize, care and support. It is understandable that people
facing a number of social problems will want to exploit a sympathetic ear. Women workers need to handle this confusion sensitively
so that people do not feel rejected but do begin to understand how
best to use the worker.

Because there is less pressure on women to 'get ahead', it is
easier for women to remain 'in the field' and/or in a particular job
for a longer period of time. This is also related to woman's
insecurity. A woman worker may need more than the average expertise
and experience before she feels sure that she is competent in an
area of work.

An event which took place in a community project I worked in
several years ago illustrates this. Five of some thirty staff
members shared areas of responsibility with the director. Three of
the five were women. When the director left the project, only the
two men considered applying for his job, in spite of the fact that
the women were on the whole older, more experienced and as well, or
better, qualified. This is not to suggest that the men should not
have considered the post or that the women should have. It is
merely to say that women are less likely to consider themselves for
top positions and less likely to move 'up' quickly.

Women's more limited ambition is a mixed blessing. Do we count
the blessing and do the work we want to do without feeling the pressure to move up the career ladder? Or are we afraid to try for the
jobs we want because of a sense of inferiority?

SUMMARY

This article has considered when women are active in community groups
and in what ways, why this is the case, and what the implications of
this are for active women and community workers, in particular
women workers.

I have tried to establish that, in spite of the influence of the
women's movement and the fact that the community is women's domain,

community development has not meant very much to women. At the
same time there are dramatic, if too few, examples of women
engaging in effective community action on their own behalf.
Ideally all community workers will address themselves to the
situation of women. But there is a particular challenge for
women community workers.

We women community workers need to incorporate into our work the
struggle for the liberation of women. A number of us are doing
this to some extent now, but we need to be doing it more consistently and explicitly. This will involve taking a position on
behalf of women in those situations in which women are restricted.
It will mean choosing to organize with women in those areas in which
women are particularly oppressed.

I feel certain that there will be accusations of bias and
'unprofessionalism' when women community workers decide to work as
women. If we are especially concerned about women are we not
neglecting our professional responsibility to the entire community?
For many of us, however, professionalism has never meant not taking
a stand. A community worker frequently decides to work with one
group or in one area rather than another because a group of people
have greater needs and are not able to organize themselves
effectively without some intervention. Enabling people to express
their concerns and to have influence over their lives is central
to community work. If women do not have full opportunity to act in
their own interest it is a community worker's job to enable them to
do so. And if groups of women do not have an equal opportunity to
act, other women need to act in solidarity to support them. We women
community workers are doubly committed.

Notes

1 B. Ashcroft and K. Jackson, Adult education and social action,
   in D. Jones and M. Mayo, eds, 'Community Work One', Routledge
   & Kegan Paul, 1974, p.47.
2 S.M. Miller and P. Roby, 'The Future of Inequality', New York,
   Basic Books, 1970, p.10.
3 The women's movement and the class struggle against patriarchy,
   in 'Women and Socialism', Conference Paper no. 3, 1974, p.21.
4 John Pitts, Conclusions, from Statistics on Crossfield
   Estate, unpublished.
5 Sir C. Buchanan and Partners, The Deptford and Greenwich Management Study, 1972.
6 Actions such as this, by council officers and members, further
   divide the better-off working-class people from those less well
   off.
7 Eleanor Macoby, 'Development of Sex Differences', Tavistock,
   1967, p.105.
8 Community participation and social change, in D. Jones and M.
   Mayo, eds, 'Community Work Two', Routledge & Kegan Paul, 1975,
   pp.28-9.
9 Merseyside Big Flame Women's Group, News, 'Spare Rib', no. 42,
   December 1975, pp.17-18.
10 ibid., p.18.

11   M. Fuller, The place of women in sociology, in Jane Chetwynd,
     ed., Proceedings from the Symposium entitled 'The Role of
     Psychology in the Propagation of Female Stereotypes', British
     Psychological Society, 1975, p.25.
12   Introduction to 'Sisterhood is Powerful', New York, Vintage
     Books, p.xx.
13   M.B. Cohen, Personal identity and sexual identity, in J.B.
     Miller, ed., 'Psychoanalysis and Women', Penguin, 1973, p.156.
14   Malcolm X, 'The worst thing the white man has done is to teach
     us to hate ourselves.'
15   Sexist ideology of casework, 'Case Con', no. 15, spring 1974,
     p.21.
16   Alvin Poussant in 'Negro Digest', November 1963, p.11.
17   'Feminine Psychology', Routledge & Kegan Paul, 1968, p.74.
18   Helen Weinreich, Women's studies, or has the female subject a
     future?, in 'The Role of Psychology in the Propagation of
     Female Stereotypes', p.32.
19   Sheila Rowbotham, 'Women's Liberation and the New Politics',
     Spokesman pamphlet no. 17, 1971, p.8.
20   Eleanor Macoby, op. cit., p.105.
21   May Fuller, op. cit., p.26.